# Cast Iron

## Cookbook for Beginners

*The Modern & Complete Collection of Recipes for Newbies to Easily & Happily Cook Countless Healthy & Tasty Dishes for Friends & Family. Unique Ideas at Any Time of the Day!*

**Lolly Selly Berry**

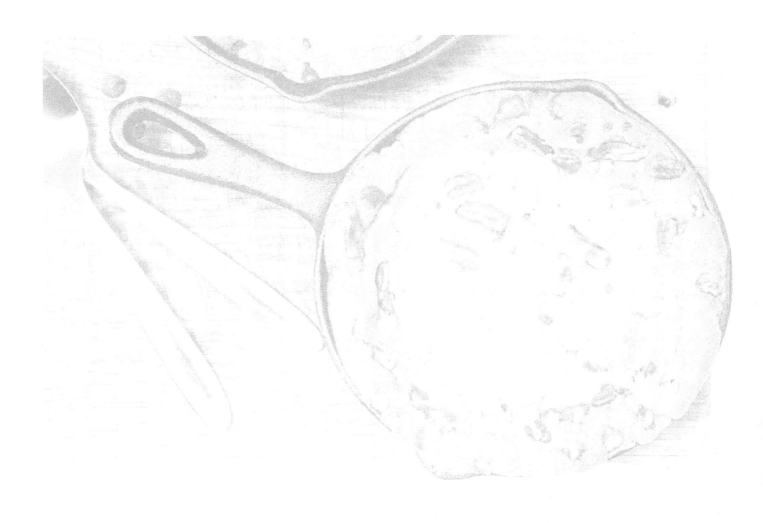

"*If you find the content of this book pleasant and the recipes tasty, I imagine your smile. At this moment, I smile too, and I can consider my work finished.*"

*Your review written on the purchasing site
of this manuscript will help me grow.*

*Anyway thanks, Lolly Selly Berry*

**Good Work!**

# TABLE OF CONTENTS

# Introduction

**A**re you ready to put your cast iron cookware to good use? If so, here's your opportunity to cook tasty and healthful foods in various cast iron pans to design your own diversified menu. Reading through this book will teach how simple it is to use a cast iron pan, but there are certain principles to follow to maximize its longevity and protect it from rusting in the long term. It is also mentioned here how to retain the cast-iron skillet's essential seasoning to keep its surface smooth and nonstick. A cast iron pan is a versatile cooking instrument that has made cooking possible by allowing you to prepare a range of cuisines. A person who enjoys cooking understands the significance of dependable cooking gear and has the least chance of rusting if properly kept; a cast iron pan is one of them. It is excellent cooking equipment when it comes to adaptability, functionality, and durability.

It may be used to prepare various foods, from vegetables to meat to sweets. Cast iron sauté pans are inexpensive and resilient, but they must be properly cared for since acidic foods may eat away at the seasoning coating. Wash it completely with hot water and soap, dry it thoroughly, apply a small amount of oil to each surface, and preheat it before cooking.

## What is a Cast Iron Pan?

Those who spend the most time in the kitchen may be familiar with the cast iron skillet as one of their cooking instruments. It is essentially a culinary tool. It has slanted edges that occasionally provide a tiny cooking surface. However, it allows you to reach the food and swirl it around the pan while cooking if necessary. Dishes cooked in a pan can also be served in the skillet itself, giving the appearance of being carefully prepared.

A cast-iron skillet is the most common form of the pan. When we hear the phrase skillet, the first thing that springs to mind is a cast iron pan. People who understand how to care for cooking utensils prefer them. You'll want to make every meal in a cast iron pan once you've become used to it!

## The Benefits of Cooking with Cast Iron Pan:

It is worthwhile to get cast iron skillets since they have several advantages.

**Nonstick:** The cast iron skillet is naturally nonstick. You must season your pan properly to maintain this degree of quality. That is the process of adding a protective coating of oil to the surface of a cast iron pan.

**All-Natural Coating:** No synthetic coatings are used to make cast iron nonstick since it can produce a nonstick surface on its own with the aid of oil.

**It is Beneficial:** Cooking on a cast iron pan may seem unusual. In fact, cooking on it is beneficial. It not only prevents contaminants from leaching from synthetic coatings, but it also protects your food from infection.

**Heat Retention:** It takes a long time to heat a cast iron pan, but it also takes longer to cool down. If you want, you may cook and serve your food in the cast iron pan since it retains heat for a longer period.

**Oven-friendly:** Cast iron has an exceptionally high heat capacity. Consequently, you may bake in it without having to worry about ruining your pan. Because they are oven-safe, cast iron skillets are perfect for slow-cooking foods and even baking. After baking cornbread or pound cake in a cast iron pan, you'll never bake it any other way! Cast iron pans will last a lifetime if properly cared for. Cast iron skillets definitely get better with usage since the porous surface smoothes out due to regular cooking with the right spatula. If the cast iron pan or skillet is not properly maintained, it can cause various problems. Because cast iron skillets are heavy because they are constructed of cast iron, they cannot be compared to the weight of stainless-steel pans and other skillets. It might be overwhelming for persons who have difficulty moving big goods. To keep iron skillets from rusting, they must be well seasoned. No matter how good you take care of your cast iron skillet, it will eventually rust. It may take some effort and time to remove the rust from the skillet, but the essential point to mention is that it can be repaired.

Because the handle is made of the same cast iron material as the skillet, a cast-iron skillet can get too hot to handle if it is left on the stove or in the oven for a longer time. As a result, caution is essential when using it to ensure the safety of the person cooking.

## Cast Iron Pan vs. Frying Pan:

Many people are perplexed by frying pans and skillets since they have many similarities, but there are also differences; they are both cooking ware products ideal for specific types of cooking. When it comes to form, there is a clear distinction between frying pans and cast iron skillets; the skillet has at least 5 cm of depth, while the frying pan is often shallower. Because the cooking techniques they're employed for don't require a lot of depth, frying pans are frequently shallower than other pans. Skillets and frying pans are roughly the same size and feature a flat bottom. Curved edges on skillets and frying pans are also equivalent. They're slightly slanted and curved, making it easy to turn food in the pan. The substance they are constructed of, on the other hand, is completely different. Aluminum pans are not long-lasting when used for high-temperature cooking. They're utilized for simple tasks like cooking eggs. Many experts utilize stainless steel pans because they are sturdy and long-lasting. Because it is nonstick, safe, and chemical-free, ceramic is also utilized to create cookware. Cast iron pans are incredibly durable and have an outstanding capacity to retain heat since this material is sturdy and used to make cookware. Cast iron is the most commonly suggested material for skillets, whereas stainless steel is chosen for frying pans. The material from which the handles are constructed is also considered since it will be difficult to hold if the handle becomes hot. As a result, hardwood handles are now utilized to prevent handles from heating up. Skillets may be used in a variety of ways in the kitchen because they are such a versatile cooking tool. The structure of the cast iron skillet makes it ideal for a variety of cooking techniques. Typically used for roasts, frittatas, stews, casseroles, and sauces, skillets may also be used for sautéing and stir-frying, provided your cooking equipment are lightweight. Cast iron skillets are heavy and difficult to shift and shake when cooking. Because of their ability to resist and sustain high cooking temperatures, cast iron pans are a fantastic choice for frying or searing food. Because of their excellent heat retention, they are an excellent choice for long-cooked, stewed dishes. When properly cared for, cast-iron skillets may acquire a nonstick surface, making them excellent for frying potatoes or cooking stir-fried dinners. Some cooks feel that cast iron is an excellent choice for egg dishes, while others say it lends an unusual flavor to the eggs. Cast-iron skillets may also be used for baking, such as making cornbread, cobblers, and pastries.

## Cast Iron Pan Sizes and Applications:

Cast iron pans come in many sizes. Which one to select is determined by the number of family members and the type of food that will be cooked in it. Cooking steak takes more room than cooking pancakes, and huge skillets will not work. In reality, three significant sizes are suitable for domestic use.

**1.      Cast Iron Pan, 8-Inch:**

Eight-inch cast iron skillets are the smallest size and are ideal for a small household of two individuals. A larger skillet is required for large objects to be cooked. The 8-inch cast-iron skillet is also known as a personal-sized pan since it may be used to make breakfast or sauté a few things. These are light in weight and may be utilized with ease. In an eight-inch skillet, you can fry two average-sized chicken thighs, one eight-ounce steak, or three or four eggs. The usefulness decreases as the size decreases. Because of their compact size, eight-inch skillets are great for things that require tossing, such as green beans or fingerling potatoes.

**2.      Cast-Iron Pan, 10-Inch:**

A 10-inch cast-iron skillet is a medium-sized pan that is ideal for a household of three to four individuals. This is the most often used size. It is a standard-sized iron skillet with a functional design. It is also the closest skillet size to a standard pie pan, so you won't have to perform any recipe translation if you want to bake in it. This skillet is perfect for most two-person dinners and whole side dishes for bigger gatherings.

### 3.    Cast-Iron Pan (12-Inch):

When cooking for a family of five to six people, twelve-inch cast iron skillets are the most common. It is particularly suggested when cooking steaks or other large pieces of meat, as well as chicken breasts. Because it is large enough, a 12-inch cast-iron skillet can cook everything in the kitchen. Though it is difficult to toss food with one hand, it is the ideal size for cooking anything.

If you make a lot of meals for your family, it is advised that you use a 12-inch skillet; this will come in useful. A 12-inch skillet is great for regularly preparing meals for four or more people. If you have a small household and rarely use a pan, a 10-inch skillet would serve.

Larger cast iron skillets than 12 inches are available in rare cases, although they are not common. Skillets greater than 12 inches in diameter are appropriate for professional use when food is prepared in large batches or groups. Most individuals will struggle to lift these extra-large cast iron skillets. Similarly, these skillets may be difficult to manage; this is why professionals recommend 8-, 10-, and 12-inch cast-iron skillets.

## Cooking On a Cast Iron Pan

Using a cast-iron skillet is fantastic! It may endure a long time if properly cared for since it is inherently nonstick and sears a crispy, caramelized coating on your meal like no other cookware. Cast iron skillets get better with age. Like much other culinary equipment, they offer several advantages; they are adaptable and may be used in a variety of ways. Cooking and cleaning a cast iron pan are easy and quick tasks.

**Preheat the Cast Iron Pan as follows:**

Before adding food, preheat your cast-iron skillet on a burner for 5-10 minutes on low to medium heat. Although cast iron pans may not always heat evenly, they are excellent at holding heat. Using a cold iron cast skillet to cook meals will never yield satisfactory results. To begin, ensure that the cast iron is warmed; if you place your palm over the pan, you should be able to feel the heat; then, for best results, add food to it.

**Add a Drop of Oil:**

Add a little oil to the cast iron skillet when it has been preheated, and then set the meal on it. Another crucial tip for using cast iron is not constantly to move the food in the pan; it must be left alone otherwise, the food will cling, and it will be difficult to turn the meal. Because cast iron is not heatproof, using an oven mitt is essential. Grab the cast iron handle with an oven mitt if you don't want to be burnt.

**Utensils that may be used with a cast iron pan:**

Cast iron is a durable and long-lasting material. If required, use metal or stainless steel spatulas. Plastic spatulas are not as lovely to use as wooden spatulas. Plastic spatulas may melt when used in cast iron pans, causing problems with your skillet and food in the long run.

Cast-iron skillets may be used to cook a variety of items such as eggs, crispy veggies, and cheese, as well as bake-off cornbread. They may also be used to sauté food. Cooking with cast iron has the advantage of allowing you to transport food from the cooktop to the oven without having to transfer it to an oven-safe dish. With only a little oil, you can cook practically anything you want to eat in a cast iron pan; you can cook steak with a crispy crust or roast an entire bird. That is why it is called magical, as it simplifies cooking for an infinite number of dishes.

## Seasoning a Cast Iron Pan

It is critical to season your cast iron pan if you do not want it to rust, lose its sheen, or be used in the long term. Seasoning takes a couple of months if the cast iron is used frequently, and it maintains the pan nonstick and smooth. It is possible to accomplish this in a few steps:

1.    Cleaning is the first step; even if the pan is fresh, it should be properly cleaned. If there is rust or food adhered to the cast iron, use dish soap to clean it. Also, good to scrub the sides, handle, and bottom of the cast iron pan with warm soapy water.

2.    After cleaning, make sure to thoroughly dry your cast iron. It's simple to do using a kitchen towel. Another method for drying cast iron is to leave the pan on the heat until the water evaporates.

3.    After drying the pan, evenly apply oil to the interior and exterior of the pan, including the handle. Excessive oil might make the pan cling.

4.      Wipe away any excess oil. The oil must be absorbed into the pores of the cast iron pan in order to create a nonstick surface: food will not adhere to it.

5.      Finally, lay the cast iron skillet upside down in the oven. Preheat the oven to 450°F/500°F, then place the pan on aluminum foil or a baking sheet for an hour.

6.      Now remove the cast iron pan from the oven and allow it to cool fully.

These are the steps for seasoning a cast iron skillet. It will smooth out the surface and make it nonstick, allowing you to cook excellent cuisine on it.

## Cleaning & Maintenance of Cast Iron Pan

### How to Clean a Cast Iron Pan

A cast iron pan is simple to clean and only a few items are required. To fully clean your skillet, all you need is hot water, a sponge, and soap. There is a requirement to remove food residue, which is difficult to remove; salt is added to the hot water and soap combination. Make careful to clean the interior, exterior, and handle of the pan.

### Taking Care of Cast Iron Pans

People who use cast iron skillets must adhere to a few guidelines in order to keep them in good condition:

1.      Cast iron skillets should not be used for marination since an acidic combination might ruin the pan's seasoning. Acidic ingredients such as tomatoes and vinegar can cause the pan seasoning to deteriorate. This does not preclude you from cooking acidic items in an iron skillet, but it does need you to season it again before cooking anything else.

2.      Avoid extreme temperature changes since they can damage your cast iron skillet. This involves submerging it in cold water soon after withdrawing it from the heat; otherwise, the pan may break.

3.      Foods with thin or fragile skin, such as fish, might become stuck to the pan and be difficult to dislodge, resulting in the ripping of the fish during turning.

4.      There's something about cast iron skillets that absorb the taste of anything you cook in them. This is perfect for cooking steaks, meats, vegetables, and other foods that benefit from the addition of different flavors. However, there is a dilemma with cooking meat in cast iron: frying brownies in it will not work; you don't want them to taste like meat! To address this issue, you will want more than one cast iron pan for cooking sweets, meats, or veggies.

5.      Add some oil to a cast iron pan and preheat it before cooking.

### How to Restore a Rusted Cast Iron Skillet

There's no need to be scared or trash your cast iron skillet if it's become rusty; it may also get oily. To get rid of it, use these basic approaches.

1.      Combine 1-2 teaspoons baking soda, 5 teaspoons salt, and 1 cup vinegar; this mixture will remove all rust.

2.      Steel wool is also used for rusty regions, but only when the iron skillet has not been seasoned.

3.      After removing the rust, thoroughly clean the cast iron pan by washing it with hot water and soap.

4.      Using dish towels, thoroughly dry the skillet.

5.      Season it once again by spreading a coating of oil to the interior, exterior, and handle of the cast iron skillet.

6.      Place the cast iron in the oven upside down. Allow it to cool before resuming cooking in it.

This restores the appearance of your skillet, but it is critical to completely dry your cast iron skillet before seasoning it.

# CHAPTER 1:

# Bread and Crepes Recipes And More

## 1. <u>Milky Cornbread</u>

*This bread is to be tried at least once. There is also a salty version by removing the sugar from the ingredients and adding enough salt*

**Difficulty Level:** Easy
**Servings:** 8
**Preparation Time:** 15 minutes
**Cooking Time:** 25 minutes
**Ingredients:**
- 1 c. cornmeal
- 1 c. flour
- ⅔ c. white sugar
- 1 tsp. salt
- 1 tbsp. baking powder
- 1 egg
- 1 c. whole milk
- ⅓ c. vegetable oil

**Directions:**
1. Preheat your oven to 400°F.
2. Lightly grease an 8-inch cast-iron wok.
3. Into a large bowl, put the cornmeal, flour, sugar, baking powder, and salt and mix well.
4. Add the egg, milk, and oil to another bowl and beat until well combined.
5. Put in the flour mixture until just combined.
6. Place the mixture into the prepared wok.
7. Bake for 20-25 minutes, or until a toothpick comes out clean.
8. From the oven, remove the wok and place it onto a wire rack to cool for at least 10 minutes.
9. Carefully invert the bread onto a platter.
10. Cut the bread into desired-sized slices with a sharp knife and serve warm.

**Nutrition (Per Serving):** Calories: 293 Fat: 12.4g Carbohydrates: 42.8g Fiber: 1.6g Sugar: 18.1g Protein: 4.6g

## 2. <u>Bran Bread</u>

*Mrs. Ellen prepares this bread once a month for her family to eat on Sunday mornings*

**Difficulty Level:** Easy
**Servings:** 6
**Preparation Time:** 15 minutes
**Cooking Time:** 22 minutes
**Ingredients:**
For the Bread:
- 1 c. all-purpose flour
- ¼ c. white sugar
- 2 tsp. baking powder
- ¼ tsp. salt
- 1 large egg
- ⅓ c. whole milk
- ¼ c. butter, melted
- 1 c. bran flakes, crushed

For the Topping:
- ⅓ c. bran flakes, crushed
- 2 tbsp. brown sugar
- 2 tsp. softened butter

**Directions:**
1. Preheat your oven to 375°F.
2. Grease an 8-inch cast iron wok.

For the Bread:
1. applenmInto a bowl, add the flour, sugar, baking powder, and salt, and mix well.
2. In another large-sized bowl, add the egg, milk, and butter and beat until well combined
3. Put in the flour mixture until just combined.
4. Add the bran flakes and mix well.

For the Topping:
5. Add everything in the ingredients list in a bowl and mix well. Place the bread mixture into prepared wok and top with the topping mixture.
6. Let it bake for 18-22 minutes or until a toothpick inserted in the center comes out clean.
7. From the oven, remove the wok and place it onto a wire rack to cool for at least 10-15 minutes.
8. Carefully invert the bread onto the rack to cool completely. Cut the bread into the desired-sized slices and serve with a sharp knife.

**Nutrition (Per Serving):** Calories: 316 Fat: 18.5g Carbohydrates: 34.8g Fiber: 1.8g Sugar: 14.2g Protein: 5g

### 3. Oat Pancakes

*⚜They are excellent pancakes for a healthy breakfast, but also for a tasty snack, as Oliver's grandmother claims⚜*

**Difficulty Level:** Easy
**Servings:** 6
**Preparation Time:** 15 minutes
**Cooking Time:** 24 minutes
**Ingredients:**
- ½ c. all-purpose flour
- 1 c. old-fashioned oats
- 2 tbsp. flaxseeds
- 1 tsp. baking soda
- Salt, as required
- 2 tbsp. agave nectar
- 2 large eggs
- 2 c. plain Greek yogurt
- 2 tbsp. extra-virgin olive oil

**Directions:**
1. In a blender, add the flour, oats, flaxseeds, baking soda, and salt and pulse until well combined.
2. Transfer the mixture into a large-sized bowl
3. All except the oil, add the remaining ingredients and mix until well combined.
4. For about 20 minutes, set aside before cooking.
5. Heat a large-sized cast-iron wok over medium heat and grease with a little oil.
6. Add ¼ c. of the mixture and cook for about 2 minutes or until the bottom becomes golden brown.
7. Carefully flip the side and cook for about 2 minutes more.
8. Repeat with the remaining mixture.

9. Serve warm.
**Nutrition (Per Serving):** Calories: 239 Fat: 9g Carbohydrates: 26.4g Fiber: 2.2g Sugar: 2.7g Protein: 13g

### 4. Tuna Omelet

*⚜You never give up on healthy food, especially if cooked in a cast iron skillet. Housewives who love good food say it⚜*

**Difficulty Level:** Easy
**Servings:** 2
**Preparation Time:** 10 minutes
**Cooking Time:** 15 minutes
**Ingredients:**
- 4 eggs
- ¼ c. unsweetened almond milk
- 1 tbsp. scallions, chopped
- 1 garlic clove, minced
- ½ of jalapeño pepper, minced
- Salt and ground black pepper, as required
- 1 (5-oz.) can water-packed tuna, drained and flaked
- 1 tbsp. unsalted butter
- 3 tbsp. green bell pepper, seeded and chopped
- 3 tbsp. tomato, chopped

**Directions:**
1. Add the eggs, almond milk, scallions, garlic, jalapeño pepper, salt, and black pepper, andbeat well in a bowl.
2. Add the tuna and stir to combine.
3. In a large-sized cast-iron frying pan, melt the butter over medium heat.
4. Place the egg mixture in an even layer and cook for about 1–2 minutes, without stirring.
5. Carefully lift the edges to run the uncooked portion flow underneath.
6. Spread the veggies over the egg mixture and sprinkle with the cheese.
7. Cover the frying pan and cook for about 30-60 seconds.
8. Remove the lid and fold the omelet in half.
9. Take away the omelet from the heat and cut it into two portions.
10. Serve immediately.
**Nutrition (Per Serving):** Calories: 232 Fat: 20.4g Carbohydrates: 3.1g Fiber: 0.7g Sugar: 1.6g Protein: 31.4g

## 5. <u>Eggs in Bell Pepper Rings</u>

*❧Always using genuine ingredients help our health and the environment❧*

**Difficulty Level:** Easy
**Servings:** 2
**Preparation Time:** 5 minutes
**Cooking Time:** 6 minutes
**Ingredients:**
- 1 green bell pepper, cut into 4 (¼-inch) rings, and seeded
- 4 eggs
- Salt and ground black pepper, as required
- 2 tbsp. fresh parsley, chopped

**Directions:**
1. Heat a large, lightly greased cast-iron wok over medium heat.
2. Place bell pepper rings in the wok and cook for about 2 minutes.
3. Flip the rings and then crack an egg in the middle of each.
4. Sprinkle each egg with salt and black pepper and cook for about 2-4 minutes or until the desired doneness of the eggs.
5. Serve with the garnishing of parsley.

**Nutrition (Per Serving):** Calories: 146 Fat: 8.9g Carbohydrates: 5.4g Fiber: 0.9g Sugar: 3.7g Protein: 11.8g

## 6. <u>Apple Pancakes</u>

*❧Good recipes are always those that are made with ingredients from nature. The apple gives the pancake a great taste❧*
*This recipe is a big pancake to be cut into wedges.*

**Difficulty Level:** Easy
**Servings:** 6
**Preparation Time:** 15 minutes
**Cooking Time:** 20 minutes
**Ingredients:**
For the Pancakes:
- 1 c. whole milk
- 3 large eggs
- ¾ c. all-purpose flour
- ½ tsp. Salt
- ⅛ tsp. ground nutmeg
- 3 tbsp. butter

For the Topping:
- 2 tart baking apples, peeled and sliced
- 3-4 tbsp. butter
- 2 tbsp. white sugar

**Directions:**
1. Preheat your oven to 425°F.
2. Place a 10-inch cast-iron wok in the oven to preheat.
3. Add the milk, eggs, flour, salt, and nutmeg in a blender and pulse until smooth.
4. Carefully remove the hot wok from the oven and add in the butter.
5. Return the wok to the oven until butter starts to bubble.
6. Place the pancake mixture into a wok over bubbling butter evenly.
7. For about 20 minutes, let it bake, or up until edges are browned and crisp.

For the Topping:
1. In a small cast-iron wok, add the apples, butter, and sugar over medium heat and cook until apples are tender, stirring frequently.
2. Place the apple mixture over the baked pancake.
3. Cut into desired-sized wedges and serve immediately.

**Nutrition (Per Serving):** Calories: 290 Fat: 17.6g Carbohydrates: 28.3g Fiber: 2.2g Sugar: 14.1g Protein: 6.4g

## 7. <u>Oats Bread</u>

⚜*The oat bread is suitable for any occasion. A recipe that you will really appreciate*⚜

**Difficulty Level:** Medium
**Servings:** 6
**Preparation Time:** 15 minutes
**Cooking Time:** 24 minutes
**Ingredients:**
For the Bread:
- 1 c. old fashioned oats
- 1 c. hot water
- ⅓ c. warm water
- 2¼ tsp. dry yeast
- ½ c. pure maple syrup
- 2 tsp. vegetable oil
- 2 tsp. salt
- 3½ c. bread flour

For the Topping:
- 1 egg, beaten lightly
- ¼ c. oats

**Directions:**
1.    Add the oats and pulse until coarse crumbs form in a food processor. Transfer the oat crumb into a large-sized bowl with hot water and mix well. Set aside until lukewarm. Add the warm water and sprinkle with yeast in the stand mixer bowl fitted with a dough hook. Set aside for about 4-5 minutes. Add the maple syrup, oil, and salt and mix well. Then put in the flour and oat mixture and mix until a soft dough forms.
2.    Place the dough onto a lightly floured surface and with your hands, knead until smooth. In a greased bowl, place the dough and turn to grease the top. Place somewhere warm and cover with plastic wrap until doubled in size. With your hands, punch down the dough well. Shape the dough into a round, smooth loaf. Arrange the dough loaf into a greased cast-iron wok. With plastic wrap, cover the wok and place it in a warm place for about 45 minutes. Preheat your oven to 350°F. Coat the bread loaf with beaten egg and sprinkle with the oats. Bake for about 30 minutes or until a toothpick inserted in the center comes out clean. From the oven, remove the wok and place it onto a wire rack to cool for at least 10-15 minutes. Carefully invert the bread onto the rack to cool completely.
3.    Cut the bread into the desired-sized slices and serve with a sharp knife.

**Nutrition (Per Serving):** Calories:  246 Fat: 2.6g Carbohydrates:  48.1g  Fiber:  2.8g   Sugar:  8.4g Protein: 2.6g

## 8. <u>Cheddar Scramble</u>

⚜*The preparation of this recipe is a bit challenging but following all the steps carefully you will achieve an excellent result*⚜

**Difficulty Level:** Hard
**Servings:** 6
**Preparation Time:** 10 minutes
**Cooking Time:** 8 minutes
**Ingredients:**
- 2 tbsp. olive oil
- 1 small yellow onion, chopped finely
- 12 large eggs, beaten lightly
- Salt and ground black pepper, as required
- 4 oz. cheddar cheese, shredded

**Directions:**
1.    Over medium heat, in a large-sized cast-iron wok, heat the oil and sauté the onion for about 4-5 minutes.
2.    Add the eggs, salt, and black pepper and cook for about 3 minutes, stirring continuously.
3.    Remove from the heat and immediately stir in the cheese.
4.    Serve immediately.

**Nutrition (Per Serving):** Calories:  264 Fat: 20.4g Carbohydrates:  2.1g  Fiber:  0.3g  Sugar:  1.4g Protein: 17.4g

## 9. <u>Sausage & Cauliflower Casserole</u>

⚜*Henry's family wants him to cook this recipe every time they visit him in his mini apartment in NYC*⚜

**Difficulty Level:** Easy
**Servings:** 8
**Preparation Time:** 10 minutes
**Cooking Time:** 1 hour 5 minutes
**Ingredients:**
- 12 oz. ground chicken sausage
- 16 oz. cauliflower florets
- 1 small red onion, chopped
- ¼ tsp. Italian seasonings
- Salt and ground black pepper, as required
- 12 large eggs

- ½ c. whole milk
- 12 oz. cheddar cheese, shredded and divided
- ½ c. mozzarella cheese, shredded

**Directions:**
1. Preheat your oven to 350°F.
2. Heat a large-sized cast-iron wok over medium-high heat and cook the sausage for about 6-8 minutes.
3. Add the cauliflower and onion and cook for about 5-7 minutes, stirring frequently.
4. In a large-sized bowl, add the eggs and milk and beat well.
5. Reserve 1 c. of cheddar cheese for topping.
6. Remove the wok from heat and drain the liquid completely.
7. Add the Italian seasoning, salt, and black pepper and stir to combine.
8. Top with the remaining cheddar cheese, followed by the mozzarella and egg mixture.
9. Gently stir the mixture and top with the reserve cheddar cheese.
10. Bake for about 40-50 minutes or until eggs are set.
11. From the oven, remove and set aside for about 5 minutes.
12. Cut into equal-sized wedges and serve.

**Nutrition (Per Serving):** Calories: 383 Fat: 26.8g Carbohydrates: 5.8g Fiber: 1.6g Sugar: 3.2g Protein: 29.8g

## 10. Caramelized Figs with Yogurt

❧*Always remember to wash the cast iron skillet after each use*❧

**Difficulty Level:** Easy
**Servings:** 4
**Preparation Time:** 10 minutes
**Cooking Time:** 7 minutes
**Ingredients:**
- 3 tbsp. honey, divided
- 8 oz. fresh figs, halved
- 2 c. plain Greek yogurt
- ¼ c. pistachios, chopped
- Pinch of ground cinnamon

**Directions:**
1. In a medium-sized cast-iron wok, add one tablespoon of the honey over medium heat and cook for about 1-2 minutes or until heated.

2. In the wok, place the figs, cut sides down, and cook for about 5 minutes or until caramelized.
3. From the heat, remove and set aside for about 2-3 minutes.
4. Divide the yogurt into serving bowls and top each with the caramelized fig halves.
5. Sprinkle with pistachios and cinnamon.
6. Drizzle each bowl with the remaining honey and serve.

**Nutrition (Per Serving):** Calories: 289 Fat: 3.8g Carbohydrates: 54.8g Fiber: 6g Sugar: 43.9g Protein: 14.2g

## 11. Chicken & Zucchini Pancakes

❧*With attention and commitment, even the most difficult recipes are made*❧

**Difficulty Level:** Hard
**Servings:** 4
**Preparation Time:** 15 minutes
**Cooking Time:** 32 minutes
**Ingredients:**
- 4 c. zucchinis, shredded
- Salt, as required
- ¼ c. cooked chicken, shredded
- ¼ c. scallion, chopped finely
- 1 egg, beaten
- ¼ c. coconut flour
- Ground black pepper, as required
- 2 tbsp. olive oil

**Directions:**
1. In a colander, place the zucchini and sprinkle with salt.
2. Set aside for about 10 minutes
3. Then squeeze the zucchini well.
4. Add the zucchini and remaining ingredients in a bowl and mix until well combined.

5. In a large-sized cast-iron wok, heat the oil over medium heat.

6. Add ¼ c. of the zucchini mixture and cook for about 3-4 minutes per side.

7. Repeat with the remaining mixture.

8. Serve warm.

**Nutrition (Per Serving):** Calories: 113 Fat: 8.7g Carbohydrates: 4.9g Fiber: 1.7g Sugar: 2.2g Protein: 5.5g

## 12. Caraway Seed Bread

*❧Cast iron is a material that retains heat, enhancing food flavors❧*

**Difficulty Level:** Hard
**Servings:** 10
**Preparation Time:** 20 minutes
**Cooking Time:** 25 minutes
**Ingredients:**
- 2 (¼-oz.) packages of active dry yeast
- 2 c. warm water, divided
- ¼ c. brown sugar
- 1 tbsp. caraway seed
- 1 tbsp. canola oil
- 2 tsp. salt
- 2¾-3¼ c. all-purpose flour, divided
- 2½ c. rye flour

**Directions:**
1. In a large-sized bowl, dissolve yeast in ½ c. of warm water.

2. Add the brown sugar, caraway seeds, oil, salt, and remaining water and mix until well combined.

3. Add one c. of all-purpose flour and rye flour beat until smooth. Add enough remaining all-purpose flour and mix until a soft dough forms.

4. Onto a floured surface, place the dough, and with your hands, knead until smooth and elastic.

5. Now, in a greased bowl, place the dough and turn to grease the top. With plastic wrap, cover the bowl and place it in a warm place for about 1 hour.

6. Punch down the dough well with your hands, and then cut it in half. Shape each dough half into a ball.

7. Arrange each dough ball in a greased 8-inch cast-iron wok. With your hands, flatten each dough ball into a 6-inch bread.

8. With plastic wrap, cover each wok and place it in a warm place for about 30 minutes. Preheat your oven to 375°F. For 25-30 minutes, bake, or until a toothpick inserted in the center comes out clean.

9. Remove the woks from the oven and place them onto a wire rack to cool for at least 10-15 minutes. Carefully invert the bread onto the rack to cool completely. Cut the bread into the desired-sized slices and serve with a sharp knife.

**Nutrition (Per Serving):** Calories: 398 Fat: 3.1g Carbohydrates: 81.3g Fiber: 9.7g Sugar: 4g Protein: 12.6g

## 13. Sourdough Bread

*❧Take care of your cast iron wok-pan. Never wash in the dishwasher❧*

**Difficulty Level:** Easy **Servings:** 10 **Preparation Time:** 25 minutes **Cooking Time:** 45 minutes
**Ingredients:**
For the Starter:
- 2 c. warm water
- 2¼ tsp. active dry yeast
- 3½ c. all-purpose flour
- 2 tbsp. white sugar

For the Bread:
- 4 c. all-purpose flour
- 2 tsp. salt
- 1¼ c. water

**Directions:**
For the Starter:
1. Place water and yeast in a glass bowl and mix until dissolved completely. Let it rest for 2-3 minutes. In the bowl of yeast mixture, place remaining ingredients and mix until well combined. Cover the bowl loosely with a kitchen wrap and set it aside in a dark place at room temperature for five days, stirring after every 12 hours. On day 5, stir the starter well.

For the Bread:
2. Place one c. of starter, flour, salt, and water in the bowl of a stand mixer and, for 10 minutes, mix at low speed. Into a large, floured bowl, place the dough and wrap with a kitchen towel. Sprinkle the top with some flour and place in a warm place for about 12 hours. Onto a floured surface, place the dough, and with your hands, knead for 3-5 minutes.

3. Now, place the dough into a bowl and sprinkle with some flour. In a warm place, place the bowl of dough for about 4 hours. Preheat your oven to 480 °F. Place the dough into a parchment paper-lined large-sized cast-iron saucepan. With a knife, score the top of the bread. With a lid, cover the pan and bake for approximately 30 minutes. Remove the lid and bake for additional 15 minutes or until a toothpick or wooden skewer inserted in the center comes out clean. From the oven, remove the loaf pan and place it onto a wire rack to cool for about 10 minutes. Put the bread upside down onto the wire rack to cool completely before slicing. Cut the bread into desired-sized slices with a sharp knife and serve.

**Nutrition (Per Serving):** Calories: 353 Fat: 1g Carbohydrates: 74.3g Fiber: 2.7g Sugar: 2.7g Protein: 10g

## 14.Simple Bread

❧*There are different types of cast iron pans, some have non-stick coatings but others must suffer a seasoning process*❧
**Difficulty Level:** Easy
**Servings:** 10
**Preparation Time:** 15 minutes
**Cooking Time:** 45 minutes
**Ingredients:**
- 3 c. + 2 tbsp. unbleached all-purpose flour
- 1¾ tsp. salt
- ½ tsp. instant yeast
- 1½ c. cool water

**Directions:**
1. Put flour, salt, and yeast into a large mixing bowl, and with a wire whisk, mix well.
2. Place the water and mix until a shaggy mixture forms.
3. With plastic wrap, cover the dough bowl and set it aside for 12-18 hours.
4. Preheat your oven to 450°F.
5. Place a cast-iron saucepan with a lid in the oven for 30 minutes.
6. Onto a generously floured surface, place the dough, and shape it into a ball.
7. With plastic wrap, cover the dough ball and set it aside for about 25-30 minutes.

8. From the oven, remove the hot pan and carefully place the dough inside.
9. Cover the pan with a lid and bake for approximately 30 minutes.
10. Remove the pan's lid and let the dough bake for additional 15 minutes. When a toothpick or (wooden) skewer inserted in the center comes out clean, the bread is done.
11. From the oven, remove the loaf pan and place it onto a wire rack to cool for about 10 minutes.
12. Now, place the bread in an inverted position onto the wire rack to cool completely before slicing.
13. Cut the bread into desired-sized slices with a sharp knife and serve.

**Nutrition (Per Serving):** Calories: 137 Fat: 0.4g Carbohydrates: 28.7g Fiber: 1.1g Sugar: 0.1g Protein: 4g

## 15.Hash Brown Casserole

❧*Cast iron allows you to cook many different recipes. This recipe is great for breakfast*❧
**Difficulty Level:** Hard
**Servings:** 8
**Preparation Time:** 15 minutes
**Cooking Time:** 1 hour 2 minutes
**Ingredients:**
- 1 lb. pork sausage
- ½ c. sweet potato, peeled and cubed
- 1 (30-oz.) package frozen shredded hash brown potatoes, thawed
- 5 large eggs, beaten lightly
- 2 c. half-and-half
- Salt and ground black pepper, as required
- 2 tbsp. olive oil
- 1½ c. cheddar cheese, shredded
- 2 c. fresh kale, tough ends removed and chopped
- ¾ c. frozen corn

**Directions:**
1. Preheat your oven to 375°F.
2. Heat a large-sized cast-iron wok over medium-high heat and cook the sausage and sweet potato for about 5-7 minutes, breaking the sausage into crumbles.
3. Transfer the sausage mixture onto a paper towel-lined plate to drain with a slotted spoon.

4. Reserve ½ c. of hash browns for topping.
5. Put the eggs, cream, salt, and black pepper into a bowl and beat until well combined.
6. Coat the bottom of another 12-inch cast-iron wok with oil. Place the remaining potatoes into the oiled wok, and with a spatula, press firmly to form an even layer. Top with the cheese, followed by the kale, corn, sausage, reserved hash browns, and egg mixture.
7. Bake for about 45-55 minutes or until eggs are set.
8. In the last 10 minutes of cooking, cover the wok loosely with a piece of foil.
9. From the oven, remove and set aside for about 5 minutes.
10. Cut into equal-sized wedges and serve.
**Nutrition (Per Serving):** Calories: 716 Fat: 47.8g Carbohydrates: 47.5g Fiber: 4.5g Sugar: 3.3g Protein: 24.2g

## 16. Eggs in Tomato Cups

❀*When they ask me what's for dinner, I answer Eggs in Tomato Cups"*❀
**Difficulty Level:** Easy
**Servings:** 4
**Preparation Time:** 15 minutes
**Cooking Time:** 17 minutes

**Ingredients:**
- 2 tbsp. olive oil
- 8 medium tomatoes
- 8 large eggs
- ¼ c. whole milk
- ¼ c. Parmesan cheese, grated
- Salt and ground black pepper, as required
- 2 tbsp. mixed fresh herbs (parsley, thyme, rosemary), chopped

**Directions:**
1. Preheat your oven to 375°F.
2. Grease a large-sized cast-iron wok with olive oil.
3. Cut all over the stems of the tomatoes with a small paring knife and then discard them.
4. With a small spoon, carefully scoop out all the seeds and pulp of the tomatoes.
5. Arrange the tomato cups into the prepared wok, cut side up in a single layer.

6. Carefully crack an egg into each tomato cup.
7. Top each egg with one tablespoon of almond milk, followed by one tablespoon of Parmesan cheese.
8. With salt and black pepper, season each egg.
9. Bake for about 15-17 minutes or until the tomatoes are tender and the egg whites are set.
10. From the oven, remove and set aside for about 5 minutes before serving.
11. Serve immediately with the garnishing of fresh herbs.
**Nutrition (Per Serving):** Calories: 274 Fat: 19g Carbohydrates: 11.5g Fiber: 3.2g Sugar: 7.9g Protein: 17.3g

## 17. Eggs in Beef Sauce

❀*The cast iron wok pan is very heavy to handle but food smells great when using it*❀
**Difficulty Level:** Easy
**Servings:** 6
**Preparation Time:** 15 minutes
**Cooking Time:** 25 minutes
**Ingredients:**
- 2 (14½-oz.) cans diced tomatoes
- 1 lb. lean ground beef
- 1 small onion, chopped finely
- 1 (4-oz.) can chopped green chiles
- 1 c. frozen corn
- Salt, as required
- 6 large eggs
- Ground black pepper, as required
- 6 tbsp. cheddar cheese, shredded

**Directions:**
1. Drain the cans of tomatoes, reserving ½ c. of juice into a bowl.
2. Heat a large-sized cast-iron wok over medium heat and cook the beef and onion for about 6-8 minutes, breaking up beef into crumbles.
3. Drain the grease from the wok.
4. Stir in the tomatoes, reserved juice, chiles, corn, and salt, and bring to a gentle simmer.
5. With a spoon, make six wells in the greens mixture.
6. Crack one egg carefully into each well and sprinkle with black pepper.

7.     With a lid, cover the wok and cook for 5-7 minutes or until egg whites are completely set.

8.     Sprinkle with cheese and immediately remove from the heat.

9.     Cover the wok for about 5 minutes before serving.

**Nutrition (Per Serving):** Calories: 298 Fat: 12.6g Carbohydrates: 13.1g Fiber: 2.6g Sugar: 6g Protein: 33.2g

## 18.Bacon & Potato Scramble

⚜*Excellent habit is to dry cast iron pan after each wash*⚜

**Difficulty Level:** Easy
**Servings:** 5
**Preparation Time:** 15 minutes
**Cooking Time:** 30 minutes
**Ingredients:**
- 8 bacon strips, chopped
- 2 c. red potatoes, chopped
- ½ c. bell pepper, seeded and chopped
- ½ c. onion, chopped
- 8 large egg
- ¼ c. whole milk
- Salt and ground black pepper, as required
- 1 c. cheddar cheese, shredded

**Directions:**
1.     Heat a 9-inch cast-iron wok over medium heat and cook the bacon for about 8-10 minutes or until crisp. Onto a paper towel-lined plate, transfer the bacon to drain with a slotted spoon.

2.     In the same wok, add the potatoes in bacon grease over medium heat and cook for about 12 minutes, stirring frequently.

3.     Put in the bell pepper and onion and cook for about 3-4 minutes. Meanwhile, add the eggs, milk, salt, and black pepper to a large-sized bowl and beat until well combined.

4.     In the wok, add the cooked bacon and stir to combine.

5.     Stir in the egg mixture and cook for about 3-4 minutes or until eggs are completely set, stirring continuously.

6.     Sprinkle with cheese and immediately remove from the heat.

7.     Cover the wok for about 5 minutes before serving.

**Nutrition (Per Serving):** Calories: 513 Fat: 35.3g Carbohydrates: 13.2g Fiber: 1.5g Sugar: 2.7g Protein: 34.6g

## 19.Salmon Scramble

⚜*There are casseroles, pots, pans, wok and many other forms of cast iron for cooking, but all adapt to the recipes, with a small skill*⚜

**Difficulty Level:** Medium
**Servings:** 1
**Preparation Time:** 10 minutes
**Cooking Time:** 5 minutes
**Ingredients:**
- 2 eggs
- 1 egg yolk
- 1 tbsp. Fresh dill, chopped finely
- ⅛ tsp. Red pepper flakes, crushed
- ⅛ tsp. garlic powder
- Salt and ground black pepper, as required
- 2 smoked salmon pieces, chopped
- 1 tbsp. olive oil

**Directions:**

1.      Add all ingredients except salmon and oil in a bowl and beat until well combined.
2.      Stir in chopped salmon.
3.      In a small cast-iron frying pan, heat the oil over medium-low heat and cook the egg mixture for about 3-5 minutes or until done completely, stirring continuously.
4.      Serve immediately.
**Nutrition (Per Serving):** Calories: 372 Fat: 29.9g Carbohydrates: 1.7g    Fiber: 0.1g    Sugar: 0.9g Protein: 24.8g

## 20. Veggies Omelet

❧*Even simple recipes can satisfy your appetite*❧
**Difficulty Level:** Easy
**Servings:** 4
**Preparation Time:** 15 minutes
**Cooking Time:** 15 minutes
**Ingredients:**
- 1 tsp. olive oil
- 2 c. fresh fennel bulbs, sliced thinly
- ¼ c. canned artichoke hearts, rinsed, drained, and chopped
- ¼ c. green olives, pitted and chopped
- 1 Roma tomato, chopped
- 6 eggs
- Salt and ground black pepper, as required
- ½ c. goat cheese, crumbled

**Directions:**
1.      Preheat your oven to 325°F.
2.      Over medium-high heat, heat the oil in a large-sized cast-iron wok and sauté the fennel bulb for about 5 minutes.
3.      Stir in the artichoke, olives, and tomato and cook for about 3 minutes.
4.      Meanwhile, add the eggs, salt, and black pepper to a bowl and beat until well combined.
5.      Place the egg mixture over the veggie mixture and stir to combine.
6.      Cook for about 2 minutes.
7.      Sprinkle with the goat cheese evenly and immediately transfer the wok into the oven.
8.      Bake for about 5 minutes or until eggs are set completely.
9.      Remove from oven and carefully transfer the omelet onto a cutting board.
10.     Cut into desired size wedges and serve.
**Nutrition (Per Serving):** Calories: 225 Fat: 15.8g

Carbohydrates:  6.6g Fiber: 2.3g    Sugar: 1.2g Protein: 15.3g

## 21. Chicken & Asparagus Frittata

❧*With the cast iron pan you can do many different types of cooking, boiled, stewed, braised, roasted and much more*❧
**Difficulty Level:** Easy
**Servings:** 4
**Preparation Time:** 15 minutes
**Cooking Time:** 12 minutes

**Ingredients:**
- ½ c. cooked chicken, chopped
- ⅓ c. Parmesan cheese, grated
- 6 eggs, beaten lightly
- Salt and ground black pepper, as required
- 1 tsp. unsalted butter
- ½ c. boiled asparagus, chopped
- 1 tbsp. fresh parsley, chopped

**Directions:**
1.      Preheat the broiler of the oven.
2.      Add in the cheese, eggs, salt, and black pepper to a bowl and beat until well combined.
3.      In a large-sized cast-iron wok, melt butter over medium-high heat and cook the chicken and asparagus for about 2-3 minutes.
4.      Add the egg mixture and stir to combine,
5.      Cook for about 4-5 minutes.
6.      Remove from the heat and sprinkle with the parsley.
7.      Now, transfer the wok under the broiler and broil for about 3-4 minutes or until slightly puffed.
8.      Cut into desired-sized wedges and serve immediately.
**Nutrition (Per Serving):** Calories:  157 Fat: 1.2g

Carbohydrates: 1.2g Fiber: 0.4g Sugar: 0.8g
Protein: 16.5g

## 22. Sausage, Bacon & Potato Frittata

*❦A quick dinner with friends with good wine and a good recipe❦*

**Difficulty Level:** Hard
**Servings:** 6
**Preparation Time:** 15 minutes
**Cooking Time:** 43 minutes
**Ingredients:**

- ½ lb. bulk pork sausage
- 6 bacon strips, chopped
- 1½ c. red potatoes, chopped finely
- 1 medium onion, chopped finely
- 8 large eggs
- 2 tsp. dried parsley flakes
- Salt and ground black pepper, as required

**Directions:**

1.    Heat a large-sized cast-iron wok over medium heat and cook the sausage for about 5-6 minutes.
2.    Transfer the sausage into a bowl. Add the bacon over medium heat and cook for about 8-10 minutes in the same wok.
3.    Onto a paper towel-lined plate, transfer the bacon to drain with a slotted spoon. Remove the grease from the wok, leaving two tablespoons inside.
4.    In the same wok, add the potatoes and onion in bacon grease over medium heat and cook for about 10-12 minutes, stirring frequently.
5.    Meanwhile, add the eggs, parsley, salt, and black pepper to a large-sized bowl and beat well.
6.    Add the cooked sausage and bacon and stir to combine in the wok. Place the egg mixture on top evenly.
7.    Cover the wok with a lid, then cook over low heat for about 8-10 minutes. Preheat your oven to the broiler. Arrange the rack about 6-inch from the heating element.
8.    Uncover the wok and broil for about 2 minutes or until eggs are set. From the oven, remove and set aside for about 5 minutes.
9.    Cut into equal-sized wedges and serve.

**Nutrition (Per Serving):** Calories: 412 Fat: 29.4g Carbohydrates: 1.7g   Fiber: 1.1g   Sugar: 1.7g
Protein: 27.3g

## 23. Spinach Frittata

*❦A few ingredients, a cast iron wok and that's it❦*

**Difficulty Level:** Easy
**Servings:** 4
**Preparation Time:** 15 minutes
**Cooking Time:** 20 minutes
**Ingredients:**

- 2 tbsp. extra-virgin olive oil
- 1 (6-oz.) bag fresh baby spinach
- 1 bunch of scallions, sliced
- Salt and ground black pepper, as required
- 8 large eggs
- 4 tbsp. whole-wheat breadcrumbs, divided
- ¾ c. water
- ½ c. feta cheese, crumbled

**Directions:**

1.    Preheat your oven to 450°F.
2.    In a medium-sized cast-iron wok, heat the oil over medium-high heat and cook the spinach and scallions for about 4 minutes, stirring frequently.  Stir in the salt and black pepper and remove from the heat.
3.    In a large-sized bowl, add the eggs, two tablespoons of breadcrumbs, water, and ½ teaspoon of salt and beat until well combined.
4.    Add the feta cheese and egg mixture into the wok and mix well.
5.    Spread the remaining breadcrumbs on top evenly.
6.    Transfer the wok into the oven and bake for about 15 minutes or until the top becomes gold.
7.    From the oven, remove and set aside for about 5 minutes.
8.    Cut into equal-sized wedges and serve.

**Nutrition (Per Serving):** Calories:  234 Fat: 17.2g Carbohydrates: 7g Fiber: 1.2g Sugar: 1.9g Protein: 14g

## 24. Eggs in Sausage & Tomato Sauce

*❦When James returns home he asks his elderly mom if he can eat some of this delicious recipe❦*

**Difficulty Level:** Easy
**Servings:** 4
**Preparation Time:** 15 minutes
**Cooking Time:** 30 minutes

**Ingredients:**
- 2 tbsp. extra-virgin olive oil
- 12 oz. hot Italian sausage links, casings removed
- 1½ c. onions, finely chopped
- 3 garlic cloves, thinly sliced
- 1 (28-oz.) can crushed tomatoes, undrained
- ¼ c. harissa paste
- 2 tsp. fresh oregano, minced
- Salt, as required
- 4 large eggs
- 4 oz. Gruyere cheese, shredded
- Ground black pepper, as required

**Directions:**
1. Preheat your oven to 375 °F.
2. Over medium-high heat, in a large-sized cast-iron wok, brown the sausage until it is almost cooked through.
3. Then add in the onions and garlic; cook and stir until onions are tender and meat is no longer pink.
4. Stir in the tomatoes, harissa paste, oregano, and salt; bring to a gentle boil, stirring constantly.
5. Reduce heat; simmer, uncovered, until slightly thickened, stirring occasionally. Carefully crack eggs into the sauce, leaving a space between each.
6. Sprinkle with cheese and black pepper, then let bake for 7-9 minutes or until egg whites and yolks are firm.
7. Serve hot.

**Nutrition (Per Serving):** Calories: 687 Fat: 47.8g Carbohydrates: 27.2g Fiber: 7.3g Sugar: 17.5g Protein: 37.6g

## 25. Shakshuka

❧*A famous and delicious recipe but after cooking, wash and dry the cast iron immediately*❧

**Difficulty Level:** Easy
**Servings:** 6
**Preparation Time:** 15 minutes
**Cooking Time:** 31 minutes
**Ingredients:**
- 2 tbsp. extra-virgin olive oil
- 1 red bell pepper, seeded and chopped
- 2 small yellow onions, chopped
- 3 garlic cloves, chopped roughly
- 1 (28-oz.) can diced tomatoes with juices
- 1 tsp. white sugar
- 1 tsp. ground coriander
- 1 tsp. ground cumin
- ¾ tsp. smoked paprika
- ¼ tsp. red pepper flakes, crushed
- 1½ tsp. salt, divided
- 2 c. fresh mixed greens (Swiss chard, kale, spinach), tough ribs removed and chopped finely
- 3 oz. feta cheese, crumbled
- 6 eggs
- ¼ c. fresh cilantro, chopped

**Directions:**
1. In a large-sized cast-iron wok, heat the oil over medium heat and cook the bell pepper, garlic, and onions for about 8 minutes, stirring frequently.
2. Stir in the tomatoes, sugar, spices, and 1¼ teaspoons of salt and cook for about 10 minutes, stirring occasionally. Stir in the greens and cook for about 5 minutes, stirring occasionally. Meanwhile, preheat the broiler of the oven. In the top position of the oven, arrange a rack. Remove the wok from the heat, and with a spoon, make six wells in the greens mixture. Carefully crack one egg into each well. Place some sauce over each egg and sprinkle the remaining salt with a spoon.
3. Place the feta around each egg evenly.
4. Place the wok over low heat and cook, covered for about 5-7 minutes or until the desired doneness of the egg whites. Now, transfer the wok into the oven and broil for about 1 minute. From the oven, remove the wok and serve hot with the garnishing of cilantro.

**Nutrition (Per Serving):** Calories: 195 Fat: 12.6g Carbohydrates: 13g Fiber: 3.3g Sugar: 7.5g Protein: 9.8g

# CHAPTER 2:

# Eggs And Red Meat Recipes

### 26. Hoisin Rib-Eye Steak

*The production of cast iron pans has not changed over the years. Some industries have a lifetime guarantee*

**Difficulty Level:** Easy
**Servings:** 3
**Preparation Time:** 10 minutes
**Cooking Time:** 10 minutes
**Ingredients:**
- 1 (1-lb.) (1¼-inch thick) rib-eye steak
- Salt and ground black pepper, as required
- 1 tbsp. canola oil
- 3 tbsp. butter
- 2 tbsp. hoisin sauce
- 1 tbsp. fresh ginger, chopped finely

**Directions:**
1. With black pepper and salt, season the steak evenly.
2. In a cast-iron wok, heat the oil over medium-high heat and cook the steak for about 3-minutes per side.
3. Stir in the butter, hoisin sauce, and ginger and cook for about 1-3 minutes, basting the steak with butter.
4. Transfer steak to cutting board onto a platter.
5. Cut the steak into slices and serve with the topping of the pan sauce.

**Nutrition (Per Serving):** Calories: 588 Fat: 50.1g Carbohydrates: 6g Fiber: 0.5g Sugar: 3g Protein: 27.4g

### 27. Eggs with Avocado and Spicy Tomatoes

*Nicholas's aunt received a cast iron skillet as a gift. Since that day she has been cooking only with this pan*

**Difficulty Level:** Hard
**Servings:** 2
**Preparation Time:** 5 minutes
**Cooking Time:** 15 minutes
**Ingredients:**
- 1 tbsp. coconut oil
- 1 10-oz. candied tomatoes with chilies (like Ro-Tel)
- 1 ripe avocado, peeled and sliced thinly
- 4 eggs, at room temperature
- Salt substitute or seasoning (like Spike), to taste
- Black pepper, to taste
- Red pepper flakes, to taste (optional)

**Directions:**
1. Preheat oven to 400°F.
2. Spread oil over cast iron skillet and place over medium heat.
3. Add tomatoes and let simmer until liquid has evaporated (about 4–5 minutes).
4. Reduce heat to low.
5. Arrange avocado slices over tomato mixture.
6. Drop-in eggs, spacing them apart, and season as desired.
7. Bake to desired doneness (about 10 minutes).
8. With red pepper flakes (if using), sprinkle, then serve.

**Nutrition (Per Serving):** Calories: 364 Carbohydrates: 10.3 g Fat: 29.9 g Protein: 14.3 g Sodium: 586 mg

### 28. Huevos Rancheros

*"A five-star recipe" is what a gourmet who loves genuine recipes says*

**Difficulty Level:** Medium
**Servings:** 4
**Preparation Time:** 15 minutes
**Cooking Time:** 15–20 minutes
**Ingredients:**
- 1 tbsp. olive oil, plus more for greasing
- ½ onion, chopped
- 2 cloves garlic, minced
- 2 tomatoes, diced, divided

- 2 c. cooked beans, rinsed
- 1 tsp. ground cumin
- 1 tsp. dried coriander
- ½ tsp. chipotle powder
- ½ tsp. smoked paprika
- Salt, to taste
- Freshly ground black pepper, to taste
- 2 tbsp. water
- 4 to 6 6-inch tortillas (enough to line cast iron pan)
- 4 eggs
- ½ c. crumbled feta or goat cheese (optional)
- 1 large avocado, sliced
- 2 tbsp. fresh cilantro, chopped
- 1 lime, cut into wedges
- Hot sauce, to taste

**Directions:**
1. Preheat oven to 400°F. Over medium heat, in a large pan, heat oil. Add onion and sauté until tender (about 5 minutes). Add garlic and sauté until fragrant (about 1–2 minutes). Add beans, spices, salt, water, and half of the tomatoes. Reduce to medium-low heat and let simmer while occasionally stirring.
2. Prepare cast iron skillet. Brush with oil and line with tortillas. The tortillas should come up the sides of the skillet. Brush tortillas with more olive oil.
3. Spread bean mixture evenly over tortillas.
4. Make four wells in the beans and drop eggs in. With salt and pepper, season to taste and sprinkle with cheese.
5. Bake until eggs are done (about 10 minutes).
6. Top with cilantro, remaining tomatoes, and avocado. Serve with lime wedges and hot sauce.

**Nutrition (Per Serving):** Calories: 530 Carbohydrates: 62.4 g Fat: 23.9 g Protein: 21.6 g Sodium: 1255 mg

## 29. Orange Glazed Steak

❧*Cooking the meat in cast iron, it is the best choice for expert cooks and beginners*❧

**Difficulty Level:** Easy
**Servings:** 3
**Preparation Time:** 10 minutes
**Cooking Time:** 15 minutes
**Ingredients:**

- 3 (6-oz.) beef top sirloin steaks
- 2 c. freshly squeezed orange juice
- 1 c. apple cider vinegar
- ½ c. Worcestershire sauce
- 3 tsp. olive oil
- 1½ tsp. steak seasoning
- Salt and ground black pepper, as required

**Directions:**
1. Mix the orange juice, cider vinegar, and Worcestershire sauce in a bowl.
2. In a single layer, place the steaks and top with the juice mixture in a large baking dish.
3. Refrigerate, uncovered, for about 45 minutes.
4. Preheat your oven to 425°F.
5. Remove the steak from the baking dish.
6. With plastic wrap, cover the steaks and set them aside at room temperature for about 15 minutes.
7. Rub the steaks with steak seasoning, salt, and black pepper generously.
8. Over high heat, in a cast-iron wok, heat the oil and cook the steaks for about 2½ minutes per side.
9. Immediately transfer the wok into the oven and bake for 8-10 minutes.
10. From the oven, remove the wok and set aside for about 5 minutes before serving.

**Nutrition (Per Serving):** Calories: 487 Fat: 15.6g Carbohydrates: 25.9g Fiber: 0.3g Sugar: 22.2g Protein: 52.7g

## 30. Eggs, Spinach & Mushrooms in a Skillet

❧*Prices of cast iron skillets range from a few dollars to several hundred dollars. The best choice is good quality, over time you will be grateful for the choice you have made*❧

**Difficulty Level:** Easy
**Servings:** 2
**Preparation Time:** 5 minutes
**Cooking Time:** 17–20 minutes
**Ingredients:**

- 1 tbsp. olive oil
- 8 oz. mini Bella mushrooms, chopped
- 2 tbsp. water
- 5 c. spinach, firmly packed
- 4 eggs, at room temperature

- 2 tbsp. butter
- Salt and pepper, to taste

**Directions:**

1. Heat the oil over medium heat in the cast iron pan.
2. Sauté the mushrooms until tender (about 8 minutes). Scoop out using a slotted spoon and transfer to a dish. Set aside.
3. Using the same skillet, add water and spinach. Cook until wilted (about 4 minutes).
4. Return the mushrooms to the skillet.
5. Season with salt and pepper.
6. Make four wells in the vegetables and add about ½ tablespoon of butter to each well.
7. Carefully drop the eggs into the wells.
8. Season the eggs with salt and pepper.
9. Cook until eggs reach desired doneness (about 5 minutes).
10. Alternatively, you may place the whole skillet under a preheated broiler and let cook until done (2–3 minutes).

**Nutrition (Per Serving):** Calories: 169 Carbohydrates: 2.8 g Fat: 14.1 g Protein: 8.4 g Sodium: 547 mg

## 31. Shakshuka (Eggs Poached in Spicy Sauce)

❧*A version of the original recipe. Grab your skillet and cook this delicious recipe idea*❧

**Difficulty Level:** Medium
**Servings:** 6
**Preparation Time:** 10 minutes
**Cooking Time:** 20 minutes
**Ingredients:**

- 2 tbsp. coconut oil
- 1 medium onion, chopped
- 1 medium bell pepper, sliced
- 4 cloves garlic, peeled and minced
- 1 tsp. sweet paprika
- ½ tsp. cumin
- ¼ tsp. red pepper flakes, or to taste
- ¼ tsp. salt
- Black pepper, to taste
- 1 28-oz. can of tomato sauce
- ¼–⅓ c. feta cheese, crumbled
- 6 eggs, at room temperature
- Parsley and mint leaves, chopped, for garnish

**Directions:**

1. Heat the oil in a cast-iron skillet over medium heat. Add onion, bell pepper, garlic, spices, salt, and pepper.
2. Until vegetables are tender, sauté (about 10 minutes). Add tomato sauce and let simmer until mixture thickens (about 10 minutes).
3. Stir in crumbled feta. Adjust the sauce's flavor with more salt, pepper, and spices, as desired.
4. Crack eggs over the sauce and drop them in, careful not to break the yolks. (You may also crack them one at a time in a bowl first and then slip each into the sauce.) Reduce heat and cover the skillet. Until egg whites are set, and yolks are done as desired, let cook (about 10 minutes).
5. Garnish with parsley and mint leaves.
6. Serve immediately with pita or any crusty bread.

**Nutrition (Per Serving):** Calories: 185 Carbohydrates: 12.9 g Fat: 11.2 g Protein: 9.4 g Sodium: 934 mg

## 32. Eggs with Crispy Potatoes and Green Beans

❧*Potatoes, green beans and eggs: carbohydrates, vegetables and proteins. A complete and healthy meal. Difficult to make? No, step by step everything takes shape*❧

**Difficulty Level:** Hard
**Servings:** 4
**Preparation Time:** 5 minutes
**Cooking Time:** 20–25 minutes
**Ingredients:**

- 1 c. fresh or cooked green beans, trimmed and cut into 1-inch pieces

- 2 tbsp. extra-virgin olive oil
- 2 lbs. raw or cooked potatoes, peeled and diced (½-inch cubes, if raw)
- 2 cloves garlic, minced
- ⅛ tsp. red pepper flakes
- ½ tsp. salt
- Freshly ground pepper, to taste
- 4 large eggs, at room temperature
- ⅛ tsp. paprika

**Directions:**
1. Steam or blanch green beans. To blanch, drop into boiling water and cook until bright green and crisp (about 3 minutes). Rinse under cold water and drain.
2. Heat oil in a cast-iron skillet over medium heat. Oil is ready when a piece of potato is dropped into it sizzles. Spread the potato slices over the skillet in a single layer. Cook, flipping over as needed, until tender inside and browned outside (about 15 minutes or less if using cooked potato).
3. Stir in blanched green beans, garlic, red pepper flakes, salt, and pepper.
4. Drop eggs over vegetables.
5. Cover and cook to desired doneness (about 3–5 minutes).
6. Sprinkle with paprika and serve.

**Nutrition (Per Serving):** Calories: 318 Carbohydrates: 42 g Fat: 12 g Protein: 12 g Sodium: 381 mg

## 33. Hash and Eggs

❧*When architect Kevin wants a healthy and nutritious breakfast he eats this recipe. It is also suitable for lunch and dinner*❧

**Difficulty Level:** Easy
**Servings:** 1–2
**Preparation Time:** 10 minutes
**Cooking Time:** 20 minutes

**Ingredients:**
- 1 small russet potato, scrubbed, unpeeled
- 1 slice bacon
- 1 tbsp. extra-virgin olive oil
- 3 c. baby spinach
- ⅛ tsp. salt
- 2 large eggs, at room temperature
- ⅔ c. shredded cheddar cheese
- Freshly ground pepper

**Directions:**
1. Prick potato all over and cook in the microwave on high (about 4 minutes). Let cool and dice.
2. Heat cast iron pan over medium-high heat and cook bacon until crisp. Remove bacon and drain over paper towel.
3. Add oil to drippings in pan and cook diced potato until browned (about 5 minutes).
4. Add the spinach and cook until wilted.
5. Make two wells in the mixture and drop eggs in.
6. Season everything with salt.
7. Cover and reduce heat. Cook partially (about 2–3 minutes).
8. Sprinkle with cheese and replace the cover. Until cheese has melted, and eggs are done, cook (about 1–2 minutes).
9. Sprinkle with chopped bacon and freshly ground black pepper.

**Nutrition (Per Serving):** Calories: 354 Carbohydrates: 25.5 g Fat: 21 g Protein: 17 g Sodium: 464 mg

## 34. Spiced Sirloin Steak

❧*Always choose to use all five senses when cooking*❧

**Difficulty Level:** Hard
**Servings:** 4
**Preparation Time:** 10 minutes
**Cooking Time:** 14 minutes
**Ingredients:**
- Oil for greasing, or cooking spray
- 1 tbsp. brown sugar
- ½ tsp. salt
- ½ tsp. ground cumin

- ½ tsp. ground coriander seeds
- ¼ tsp. ground red pepper
- 1 lb. boneless sirloin steak (about 1¼ inches thick), trimmed

**Directions:**
1. Preheat oven to 450°F.
2. Grease cast iron skillet.
3. For around 5 minutes, place the pan in the oven.
4. Meanwhile, combine brown sugar, salt, and spices and rub evenly over the steak.
5. Place steak in preheated pan.
6. Bake to desired doneness (about 7 minutes on each side).
7. Let stand for 3–5 minutes before slicing.

**Nutrition (Per Serving):** Calories: 198 Carbohydrates: 3.7 g Fat: 8.6 g Protein: 25.1 g Sodium: 350 mg

## 35. Strip Steaks with Smoky Cilantro Sauce & Roasted Vegetables

⚜ *"This recipe is always worth cooking" this is what William's wife always says, who is satisfied with the result* ⚜

**Difficulty Level:** Easy **Servings:** 4 **Preparation Time:** 10 minutes **Cooking Time:** 20 minutes
**Ingredients:**
- 2 8-oz. strip steaks, trimmed and halved
- 1 tbsp. extra virgin olive oil
- ½ tsp. salt
- ½ tsp. black pepper

For the Vegetables:
- 2 tbsp. extra virgin olive oil
- 1 lb. Brussels sprouts, trimmed and quartered
- 1 large sweet potato, peeled and cubed
- ¼ tsp. salt
- ¼ tsp. ground pepper

For the Sauce:
- 2 tbsp. extra virgin olive oil
- ½ tsp. brown sugar
- 1 c. packed fresh cilantro
- 1 small fresh red chili, seeded and chopped
- 1 large clove garlic, finely grated
- 1 tbsp. tomato paste
- 2 tsp. red-wine vinegar
- 1 tsp. smoked paprika
- ½ tsp. ground cumin

**Directions:**
1. Preheat oven to 450°F. In a blender or food processor, place ingredients for the sauce and pulse to make a puree. Set aside. To prepare vegetables, heat cast iron pan over high heat. Swirl in the oil and reduce heat to medium. Add vegetables and season with salt and pepper. Sauté until vegetables are half-cooked (about 10 minutes). Use a slotted spoon to transfer to a plate. Set aside. Add the oil for the steaks to the skillet to heat. Season the steaks and cook to brown (1 minute on both sides). Add the vegetables to the skillet with the steaks. Pour about half of the sauce over the steaks. Place in oven and bake to desired doneness (about 8–10 minutes; 140°F internal temperature for medium-rare and 155°F for medium-well). Remove from heat.
2. Stir remaining sauce into vegetables. Serve.

**Nutrition (Per Serving):** Calories: 399 Carbohydrates: 22 g Fat: 23 g Protein: 27 g Sodium: 559 mg

## 36. Beef Tenderloin Steaks and Balsamic Green Beans

⚜ *Cast iron pans do not fear any cooking and are eternal* ⚜

**Difficulty Level:** Easy
**Servings:** 4
**Preparation Time:** 5 minutes
**Cooking Time:** 25 minutes
**Ingredients:**
- 2 tsp. butter, divided
- 2 large yellow onions, sliced
- 3 garlic cloves, minced
- ½ c. beef broth
- 2 c. green beans, trimmed
- 2 tbsp. balsamic vinegar
- ¼ tsp. salt, divided
- 1 tsp. coconut oil or cooking spray
- 4 4-oz. beef tenderloin steaks
- ¼ tsp. freshly ground black pepper

**Directions:**
1. Melt one teaspoon butter in a saucepan over medium-high heat.
2. Add onions and sauté until translucent (about 5 minutes).
3. Add garlic and sauté until fragrant (about 1 minute).

4. Stir in broth and cook until reduced (about 4 minutes).

5. Add beans and stir until bright green (about 2 minutes).

6. Add balsamic vinegar, cover, and cook until beans are crisp-tender (about 3 minutes).

7. Turn off heat and stir in remaining butter.

8. Sprinkle with ⅛ teaspoon salt.

9. Meanwhile, season steaks with remaining salt and pepper.

10. Heat cast-iron skillet over medium-high heat.

11. Swirl in oil or spray with cooking spray.

12. Cook steaks to desired doneness (about 3 minutes per side).

13. Turn off heat and let stand for 5 minutes.

14. Serve with bean mixture.

**Nutrition (Per Serving):** Calories: 244 Carbohydrates: 12.4 g Fat: 9.4 g Protein: 27.1 g Sodium: 285 mg

## 37. Steak with Glazed Carrots & Turnips

⚜Cooking is an art but using cast iron turns it into poetry⚜

**Difficulty Level:** Hard
**Servings:** 4
**Preparation Time:** 5 minutes
**Cooking Time:** 20–25 minutes
**Ingredients:**

- 2 tbsp. extra-virgin olive oil, divided
- 1 tbsp. butter
- 1 lb. small carrots, halved lengthwise
- 3 medium turnips, peeled and cut into thick matchsticks
- ¾ tsp. salt, divided
- ¾ tsp. ground pepper, divided
- 1 lb. sirloin steak, about 1 inch thick, trimmed and halved crosswise
- 1 tsp. minced fresh rosemary or ½ teaspoon dried rosemary
- 2 tbsp. brown sugar
- 1 tbsp. red-wine vinegar

**Directions:**

1. Preheat oven to 450°F.

2. Season steak pieces with ½ teaspoon each of salt and pepper plus the rosemary. Set aside. Heat cast-iron skillet over medium-high heat.

3. Add one tablespoon oil plus butter.

4. Add carrots and turnips.

5. Sprinkle with ¼ teaspoon each of salt and pepper. Sauté until browned and beginning to soften (about 10 minutes). Use a slotted spoon to transfer veggies to a plate. Add the remaining oil to the skillet and heat to almost smoking.

6. Sear the steak (2 minutes on both sides).

7. Return the veggies to the skillet with the steak. Stir brown sugar into the veggies.

8. Bake until steak reaches desired doneness (about 8 minutes; 140°F internal temperature for medium-rare and 155°F for medium-well).

9. Transfer steak to a chopping board and rest for 5 minutes before slicing.

10. Stir vinegar into vegetables.

11. Slice steak and serve with vegetables.

**Nutrition (Per Serving):** Calories: 328 Carbohydrates: 25 g Fat: 15 g Protein: 24 g Sodium: 639 mg

## 38. Steak with Chermoula

⚜What to say about this recipe: simply delicious⚜

**Difficulty Level:** Hard
**Servings:** 6
**Preparation Time:** 5–10 minutes
**Cooking Time:** 8 minutes
**Ingredients:**
For the Chermoula:

- 1 c. fresh parsley leaves
- 1 c. fresh cilantro leaves
- 1 tbsp. paprika
- 3 tbsp. beef broth
- 2 tbsp. fresh lime juice
- 1 tbsp. olive oil
- 1 tsp. ground cumin
- ½ tsp. ground coriander
- ¼ tsp. salt
- ¼ tsp. ground red pepper
- 4 garlic cloves, peeled

For the Steak:

- 1 1½-lb. flank steak, trimmed
- ¼ tsp. salt
- ¼ tsp. freshly ground black pepper
- Cooking spray or cooking oil for greasing

**Directions:**

1.	Prepare chermoula by adding ingredients to a blender or food processor. Pulse until a paste is formed. Set aside. Season the steaks with salt and pepper. Heat cast-iron skillet over high heat.

2.	Spray with cooking spray or swirl with oil.

3.	Cook steak for 4 minutes on one side. Flip over and cook to desired doneness (about 4 minutes for medium-rare). Using a thermometer, the internal temperature should be 140°F for medium-rare and 155°F for medium-well. Let rest for 5 minutes before slicing. Serve with chermoula.

**Nutrition (Per Serving):** Calories: 195 Carbohydrates: 2.6 g Fat: 8.9 g Protein: 25.3 g Sodium: 284 mg

## 39. Cast-Iron Burgers

⚜*Water and baking soda help eliminate rust in cast iron*⚜

**Difficulty Level:** Easy

**Servings:** 4 **Preparation Time:** 20 minutes plus 30 minutes refrigeration **Cooking Time:** 25–30 minutes

**Ingredients:**

For the Patties:
- 1 lb. ground sirloin
- ½ tsp. salt
- Horseradish spread:
- 1 tbsp. canola mayonnaise
- 1 tbsp. Dijon mustard
- 1 tbsp. prepared horseradish
- 2 tsp. ketchup

For the Relish:
- 2 slices applewood-smoked bacon, chopped
- 3 c. vertically sliced yellow onion
- 1 tbsp. finely chopped chives
- 1 tsp. Worcestershire sauce
- ¼ tsp. freshly ground black pepper

Remaining Ingredients:
- Cooking spray
- 4 1½-oz. hamburger buns or Kaiser rolls
- 4 thick tomato slices
- 1 c. lettuce, shredded

**Directions:**

1.	Divide the ground sirloin into four portions. Pat them lightly together to make four ½-inch thick patties.

2.	Sprinkle with salt and refrigerate for 30 minutes. Mix ingredients for horseradish spread together in a small bowl. Set aside.

3.	To make relish, first place bacon in a cast-iron skillet. Place on the stovetop over low heat. Let bacon cook slowly until it begins to curl. Flip over several times until evenly crisp. Remove from skillet and drain over paper towels, to be chopped after draining. Cook the onions in the same skillet, using the bacon drippings, until browned (about 15 minutes). Transfer to a bowl along with other relish ingredients and chopped bacon. Set aside. To cook patties, heat a clean cast-iron skillet over medium-high heat. Spray or grease with cooking oil. Add the patties and cook to desired doneness (about 2–3 minutes on each side).

4.	To assemble a burger, spread horseradish sauce over the insides of a hamburger bun. Add a patty and top with relish, a slice of tomato, and shredded cabbage. Repeat for the rest of the buns.

**Nutrition (Per Serving):** Calories: 351 Carbohydrates: 32.7 g Fat: 12 g Protein: 29.2 g Sodium: 788 mg

## 40. Fajitas with Chimichurri

⚜*Cast iron pans have a natural non-stick film that improves over time with a lot of use*⚜

**Difficulty Level:** Medium

**Servings:** 6

**Preparation Time:** 15 minutes plus 1-hour marinating time **Cooking Time:** 15 minutes

**Ingredients:**
- 1½ lbs. flank steak, cut into three pieces
- 1 tbsp. olive oil
- 1 red bell pepper, seeded and sliced
- 1 yellow pepper, seeded and sliced

- 1 poblano pepper, seeded and sliced
- 6–8 flour tortillas, warmed
- Queso fresco or cotija cheese, crumbled
- Guacamole or sliced avocado, for serving

For the Steak Marinade:
- 3 tbsp. olive oil
- 1 tsp. chili powder
- 1 tsp. smoked paprika
- ½ tsp. cumin
- Zest and juice of 2 limes
- Salt and pepper, to taste

For the Chimichurri:
- 1 c. fresh cilantro, chopped finely
- 1 c. fresh parsley, chopped finely
- 1–2 jalapenos or Serrano chilies, seeded and chopped
- 4 cloves garlic, minced
- ½ c. olive oil
- 2 tbsp. red wine vinegar
- Salt, to taste

For the Cucumber Salsa:
- 1 cucumber, diced
- 1 mango, peeled and diced
- Juice of 2 limes
- ⅓ c. fresh cilantro, chopped
- 1–2 jalapenos, seeded and chopped
- Salt, to taste

**Directions:**

1. Combine the marinade ingredients in a shallow container or large Ziploc bag. Marinate the steak, refrigerate for 1 hour to overnight.
2. For chimichurri sauce, mix the ingredients well in a bowl. Cover and refrigerate.
3. For the cucumber salsa, toss ingredients together, cover, and refrigerate.
4. To prepare steak fajitas, heat a large cast-iron skillet over medium-high heat. Add olive oil, peppers, salt, and pepper. Stir-fry until fragrant and tender (about 4–5 minutes). Using a slotted spoon, remove the pepper mixture from the skillet. Reheat the skillet and sear the steak on one side (about 3 minutes). Flip over and cook until the steak reaches your desired doneness (about 4–5 minutes). Remove from the heat and let rest for 5 minutes. Slice, against the grain, into strips.
5. To assemble, fill a tortilla with steak and peppers, drizzle with chimichurri sauce, and top with salsa and cheese.

**Nutrition (Per Serving):** Calories: 407 Carbohydrates: 19.2 g Fat: 21.5 g Protein: 35.5 g Sodium: 122 mg

## 41. Moroccan Steak with Roasted Pepper Couscous

❧Spicy Moroccan flavors with steak are accompanied by roasted peppers and couscous❧

**Difficulty Level:** Easy **Servings:** 4 **Preparation Time:** 5 minutes **Cooking Time:** 20 minutes

**Ingredients:**
- 2 medium bell peppers
- 1 lb. skirt steak or sirloin steak, about 1 inch thick, trimmed
- 1 tbsp. extra-virgin olive oil
- Lemon wedges, for garnish

For the Couscous Mixture:
- 1 tsp. spice mix (see below)
- 1 tsp. extra-virgin olive oil
- Juice of 1 lemon
- Zest of ½ lemon
- ¾ c. water
- ⅔ c. whole-wheat couscous
- 2 tbsp. green olives, chopped

For the Spice Mix:
- 1 tsp. ground cumin
- 1 tsp. ground coriander
- ¾ tsp. salt
- ½ tsp. ground turmeric
- ½ tsp. ground cinnamon
- ½ tsp, freshly ground pepper

**Directions:**

1. Preheat broiler. Roast bell peppers under the broiler until tender, with surface charred (about 10–15 minutes). Flip over occasionally for even roasting. Let cool and then chop. Set aside (to be mixed with couscous later).
2. Meanwhile, combine ingredients for the spice mix. Separate one teaspoon for couscous and rub the rest over the steak. Let stand.
3. Prepare couscous. Take one teaspoon of the spice mix in a saucepan and combine with lemon zest and juice.
4. Add water and bring to a boil. Stir in couscous and remove from heat. Cover and let cool slightly.
5. Stir in olives and peppers.
6. Set aside.

7.	Heat cast-iron skillet over medium-high heat. Swirl in oil and heat until oil shimmers.

8.	Cook the steak to desired doneness (about 2–3 minutes on each side for medium-rare; 140°F internal temperature for medium-rare and 155°F for medium-well).

9.	Let stand for 5 minutes before slicing. Serve immediately with couscous and lemon wedges. **Nutrition (Per Serving):** Calories: 454 Carbohydrates: 36 g Fat: 18 g Protein: 36 g Sodium: 663 mg

## 42. Tomatoes Braised Beef

❧*The grandmothers, once to clean the cast iron pan, boiled water and salt inside it*❧

**Difficulty Level:** Hard
**Servings:** 10
**Preparation Time:** 10 minutes
**Cooking Time:** 1 hour 55 minutes
**Ingredients:**
- ¼ c. vegetable oil
- 3 lbs. boneless beef chuck roast, cut into 1½-inch cube
- 3 celery stalks, chopped
- 2 onions, chopped
- 4 garlic cloves, minced
- 2 (28-oz.) cans of Italian-style stewed tomatoes
- 1 c. dry red wine
- ½ c. fresh parsley, chopped
- Salt and ground black pepper, as required

**Directions:**
1.	In a large-sized cast-iron saucepan, heat the oil over medium-high heat and sear the beef cubes for about 4-5 minutes.
2.	Add the celery, onions, and garlic and cook for about 5 minutes, stirring frequently.
3.	Stir in the remaining ingredients and bring to a boil.
4.	Reduce heat to low and simmer, covered for about 1½-1¾ hours or until the desired doneness of beef.
5.	Serve hot.
**Nutrition (Per Serving):** Calories: 450 Fat: 23.7g Carbohydrates: 9.6g Fiber: 2.6g Sugar: 5.4g Protein: 44.1g

## 43. Glazed Filet Mignon

❧*As you cook, imagine the food taking shape. Cooking is creativity*❧

**Difficulty Level:** Medium
**Servings:** 2
**Preparation Time:** 10 minutes
**Cooking Time:** 12 minutes
**Ingredients:**
- 2 (4-oz.) fillet mignon
- Salt and ground black pepper, as required
- ¼ c. dry red wine
- ¼ c. balsamic vinegar

**Directions:**
1.	Rub the filet mignon with salt and black pepper generously.
2.	Heat a medium-sized cast-iron wok over medium-high heat and cook filets for about 1-2 minutes per side or until browned.
3.	Add wine and vinegar and immediately adjust the heat to medium-low.
4.	Cover and cook for about 4 minutes.
5.	Flip the filets and baste with pan sauce.
6.	Cover and cook for about 4 minutes more.
7.	Transfer the steaks to serving plates.
8.	Top with pan glaze and serve immediately.
**Nutrition (Per Serving):** Calories: 268 Fat: 10.8g Carbohydrates: 1.1g Fiber: 0g Sugar: 0.4g Protein: 32.4g

## 44. Steak with Green Veggies

*❧This good recipe is chosen by those who want healthy cooking❧*

**Difficulty Level:** Medium
**Servings:** 5
**Preparation Time:** 20 minutes
**Cooking Time:** 25 minutes
**Ingredients:**

- 1 garlic clove, grated
- ⅓ c. + 3 tbsp. olive oil
- ⅓ c. Dijon mustard
- 1 tbsp. red wine vinegar
- 1 tbsp. water
- 1 tsp. Honey
- ⅛ tsp. cayenne pepper
- Salt and ground black pepper, as required
- 1 lb. boneless New York strip steak, patted dry
- 1 bunch of scallions, sliced thinly and divided
- 4 garlic cloves, sliced
- 1 (10-oz.) bag frozen green peas
- 1 lb. asparagus, trimmed and cut into 1-inch pieces

**Directions:**

1. In a bowl, add one grated garlic clove, ¼ c. of oil, mustard, vinegar, water, honey, cayenne pepper, salt, and black pepper, and beat until well combined. Set aside. Season steak with salt and black pepper evenly and then coat with one tablespoon of oil
2. Heat a large cast-iron wok over medium-high heat and cook the steak for about 10-12 minutes, flipping after every 2 minutes.
3. With a slotted spoon, transfer the steak onto a plate. Remove the oil from the wok, leaving crispy bits behind. Heat the remaining oil over low heat in the same wok and sauté the scallion and garlic slices for about 3 minutes. Add green peas and a splash of water and cook for about 5 minutes, stirring occasionally.
4. Add the asparagus, salt, and black pepper and cook for about 5 minutes, stirring occasionally.
5. Meanwhile, cut the steak into desired-sized slices. Stir in the steak slices and remove from the heat.
6. Transfer the steak mixture onto serving plates and drizzle with some mustard sauce.
7. Serve alongside the remaining mustard sauce.

**Nutrition (Per Serving):**
Calories: 472 Fat: 34.2g Carbohydrates: 15.4g Fiber: 5.9g Sugar: 5.9g Protein: 30.3g

## 45. Beef, Mango & Veggie Curry

*❧When the recipe seems difficult to you, follow the step-by-step directions and imagine it❧*

**Difficulty Level:** Medium
**Servings:** 5
**Preparation Time:** 20 minutes
**Cooking Time:** 25 minutes
**Ingredients:**

- 14 oz. sirloin steak, trimmed and sliced thinly
- Salt and ground black pepper, as required
- 2 tsp. olive oil
- 2 tbsp. red curry paste
- 3 bell peppers, seeded and cut into 2-inch thin strips
- 1 lb. fresh green beans, trimmed and cut into 2-inch pieces
- 14 oz. plain Greek yogurt, whipped
- ¼ c. water
- 1 c. mango, peeled, pitted, and cubed

**Directions:**

1. Season the beef slices with salt and black pepper evenly
2. In a large cast-iron wok, heat the oil over medium-high heat and cook the beef for about 5-6 minutes or until browned from all sides.
3. With a slotted spoon, transfer the beef strips into a bowl
4. In the same wok, add the curry paste over medium heat and sauté for about 1 minute
5. Add the bell peppers and green beans and cook for about 3-4 minutes, stirring frequently.
6. Stir in the yogurt and water and bring to a gentle boil.
7. Cover the wok and cook for about 5-7 minutes.
8. Stir in the mango, cook beef, and cook for about 2-3 minutes.
9. Serve hot.

**Nutrition (Per Serving):** Calories: 314 Fat: 10.1g Carbohydrates: 21.2g Fiber: 4.6g Sugar: 11.8g Protein: 34.8g

## 46.Short Ribs with Veggies

*⚜In the past, housewives used cast iron a lot for cooking and the cooking was healthy⚜*

**Difficulty Level:** Medium
**Servings:** 3
**Preparation Time:** 15 minutes
**Cooking Time:** 30 minutes
**Ingredients:**
- 1 lb. boneless beef short ribs, sliced thinly against the grain
- Salt and ground black pepper, as required
- 3 tbsp. sesame oil, toasted
- 8 oz. shiitake mushrooms, sliced thinly
- 2 small onions, sliced thinly
- 1 bunch of scallions, cut into 1-inch pieces
- ½ tsp. fresh ginger, grated
- 4 garlic cloves, grated
- ¼ c. sambal oelek
- 1 tbsp. mirin
- 6 oz. snow peas
- 6 medium radishes, trimmed, quartered
- 1 c. low-sodium chicken broth

**Directions:**
1. Season the beef ribs with salt and black pepper evenly.
2. Season the beef ribs with salt and black pepper evenly.
3. Heat the oil over high heat in a large cast-iron wok and cook the beef ribs for about 8-10 minutes, stirring occasionally.
4. Add the mushrooms and onions and cook for about 6-8 minutes, stirring occasionally.
5. Stir in the scallions, ginger, and garlic and cook for about 2 minutes, stirring continuously.
6. Stir in the sambal oelek and mirin and cook for about 1 minute, stirring continuously.
7. Stir in the snow peas, radishes, and broth and bring to a boil.
8. Cook for about 5 minutes.
9. Serve hot.

**Nutrition (Per Serving):** Calories: 512 Fat: 23.5g Carbohydrates: 24.6g Fiber: 4.9g Sugar: 9.1g Protein: 50.7g

## 47.Ground Beef with Mushrooms

*⚜Mushrooms with Ground Beef, a pairing to try and easy to make⚜*

**Difficulty Level:** Easy
**Servings:** 4
**Preparation Time:** 15 minutes
**Cooking Time:** 25 minutes
**Ingredients:**
- 1 lb. lean ground beef
- 2 tbsp. olive oil
- 2 garlic cloves, minced
- ½ of yellow onion, chopped
- 2 c. fresh mushrooms, sliced
- 2 tbsp. fresh basil
- ¼ c. beef broth
- 2 tbsp. balsamic vinegar
- 2 tbsp. fresh parsley, chopped

**Directions:**
1. Heat a large-sized cast-iron wok over medium-high heat and cook the ground beef for about 8-10 minutes, breaking up the chunks with a wooden spoon.
2. With a slotted spoon, transfer the beef into a bowl.
3. Add the onion and garlic for about 3 minutes in the same wok.
4. Add the mushrooms and cook for about 5-7 minutes.
5. Add the cooked beef, basil, broth, and vinegar and bring to a boil.
6. Adjust the heat to medium-low and simmer for about 3 minutes.
7. Stir in parsley and serve immediately.

**Nutrition (Per Serving):** Calories: 289 Fat: 14.2g Carbohydrates: 3.2g Fiber: 0.8g Sugar: 1.3g Protein: 36g

# 48. Pork Chops in Mushroom Sauce

*The meat cooked in cast iron keeps the exalted flavors and aromas intact*

**Difficulty Level:** Medium
**Servings:** 4
**Preparation Time:** 15 minutes
**Cooking Time:** 35 minutes
**Ingredients:**
- 1 tbsp. olive oil
- 4 large boneless rib pork chops
- 1 tsp. salt
- 1 c. fresh mushrooms, sliced
- 3 tbsp. yellow onion, chopped finely
- 2 tbsp. fresh rosemary, chopped
- ⅓ c. homemade chicken broth
- 1 tbsp. Dijon mustard
- 1 tbsp. unsalted butter
- ⅔ c. heavy cream
- 2 tbsp. sour cream

**Directions:**
1. Heat the oil in a large-sized cast-iron wok over medium heat and sear the chops with the salt for about 3-4 minutes or until browned completely.
2. Transfer the pork chops onto a plate with a slotted spoon and set them aside.
3. Add the mushrooms, onion, rosemary, and sauté for about 3 minutes in the same wok.
4. Stir in the cooked chops, broth and bring to a boil.
5. Adjust the heat to low and cook, covered for about 20 minutes.
6. Transfer the pork chops onto a plate with a slotted spoon and set them aside.
7. In the same wok, stir in the butter until melted.
8. Add the heavy cream and sour cream and stir until smooth.
9. Stir in the cooked pork chops and cook for about 2-3 minutes or heated completely.
10. Serve hot.

**Nutrition (Per Serving):** Calories: 439 Fat: 22.6g Carbohydrates: 3.5g Fiber: 1.2g Sugar: 0.7g Protein: 53.8g

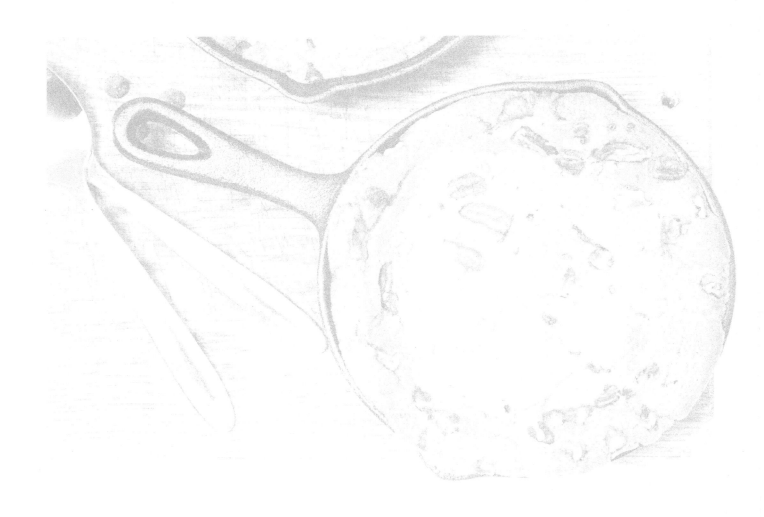

# CHAPTER 3:

## Poultry Recipes

## 49. Simple Chicken Thighs

*Few ingredients, but these chicken thighs are really excellent*

**Difficulty Level:** Hard
**Servings:** 6
**Preparation Time:** 10 minutes
**Cooking Time:** 22 minutes
**Ingredients:**
- 6 (6-oz.) skin-on, bone-in chicken thighs
- Salt and ground black pepper, as required
- 1 tbsp. vegetable oil

**Directions:**
1. Preheat your oven to 475°F.
2. Season the chicken thighs with salt and black pepper evenly.
3. In a 12-inch cast-iron wok, heat the oil over high heat.
4. Place the chicken thighs, skin side down, and cook for about 2 minutes in the wok.
5. Now, place the chicken thighs, skin side down, and cook for about 2 minutes, flipping occasionally.
6. Transfer wok into the oven and bake for about 13 minutes.
7. Flip the chicken thighs and bake for about 5 minutes.
8. Serve hot.

**Nutrition (Per Serving):** Calories: 294 Fat: 12.7g Carbohydrates: 0g Fiber: 0g Sugar: 0g Protein: 42.4g

## 50. Parmesan Chicken Thighs

*On the first Tuesday of each month, Evelyn's grandmother prepares this favorite recipe for her granddaughter who goes to dinner at her house*

**Difficulty Level:** Medium
**Servings:** 6
**Preparation Time:** 15 minutes
**Cooking Time:** 30 minutes
**Ingredients:**
- 6 (6-oz.) skin-on chicken thighs, trimmed
- 1 tsp. olive oil
- 1 tbsp. Parmesan cheese, grated
- 1 garlic clove, minced
- 1 tbsp. dried basil
- Salt, as required
- Pinch of ground black pepper

**Directions:**
1. Preheat your oven to 450°F.
2. With your hands, carefully create a pocket between the skin and thigh meat
3. Add a few drops of oil and remaining ingredients in a bowl and mix until well combined.
4. Stuff the pocket of each thigh with Parmesan mixture evenly
5. In a cast-iron wok, heat the remaining oil over medium-high heat.
6. Place chicken thighs, skin side down, and cook for about 5 minutes
7. Carefully flip the thighs and cook for about 8-10 minutes.
8. Place the wok in the oven and bake for about 15-20 minutes or until the desired doneness of the chicken. Remove from oven and set aside for about 5-10 minutes before serving.

**Nutrition (Per Serving):** Calories: 334 Fat: 13.1g Carbohydrates: 0.2g Fiber: 0g Sugar: 0g Protein: 49.4g

## 51. Chicken with Fig Sauce

*Nice recipe with unmistakable flavors*

**Difficulty Level:** Hard
**Servings:** 4
**Preparation Time:** 15 minutes
**Cooking Time:** 20 minutes
**Ingredients:**
- 4 (6-oz.) skinless, boneless chicken breast halves

- 1½ tbsp. Fresh thyme leaves, chopped and divided
- ½ tsp. Salt, divided
- ¼ tsp. ground black pepper
- 2 tbsp. olive oil, divided
- ¾ c. onion, chopped
- ½ c. dried figs, chopped finely
- ½ c. chicken broth
- ¼ c. balsamic vinegar
- 2 tsp. low-sodium soy sauce

**Directions:**
1. Season the chicken breast halves with 1½ teaspoons of thyme, ¼ teaspoon of salt, and black pepper evenly.
2. In a large-sized cast-iron wok, heat one tablespoon of oil over medium-high heat and cook the chicken for about 6 minutes per side or until done completely.
3. With a slotted spoon, transfer the chicken onto a plate, and with a piece of foil, cover to keep warm.
4. Heat the remaining oil over medium heat in the same wok and sauté the onion for about 3 minutes.
5. Stir in the figs, broth, vinegar, and soy sauce and simmer for about 3 minutes.
6. Stir in the remaining thyme and salt and remove from the heat.
7. Cut each chicken breast halves into long slices diagonally.
8. Serve the chicken slices with the topping of fig sauce.

**Nutrition (Per Serving):** Calories: 355 Fat: 13.6g Carbohydrates: 19.1g Fiber: 3.3g Sugar: 13.2g Protein: 39.9g

## 52. Turkey with Mushrooms

⚜Cooking with a cast iron pan is an excellent habit⚜

**Difficulty Level:** Easy
**Servings:** 2
**Preparation Time:** 15 minutes
**Cooking Time:** 20 minutes
**Ingredient:**
- 1 tbsp. butter
- 1 garlic clove, minced
- ½ lb. boneless skinless turkey breast, cut into 2-inch strips

- 2 c. fresh mushrooms, sliced
- ¾ c. beef broth
- 1 tbsp. Tomato paste
- ⅛ tsp. salt

**Directions:**
1. In a large-sized cast-iron wok, melt butter over medium heat and sauté the garlic for about 1 minute.
2. Add turkey and cook for about 5-6 minutes or cooked through.
3. With a slotted spoon, transfer the turkey strips onto a plate.
4. Add the mushrooms and cook for about 4-6 minutes in the same wok.
5. Add the broth, tomato paste, and salt and cook for about 3-5 minutes, stirring occasionally.
6. Stir in the cooked turkey strips and cook for about 2-3 minutes.
7. Serve hot.

**Nutrition (Per Serving):** Calories: 199 Fat: 7g Carbohydrates: 4.7g Fiber: 1.1g Sugar: 2.5g Protein: 32.6g

## 53. Chicken with Capers Sauce

⚜Cooking is creation. Each recipe is a work of art⚜

**Difficulty Level:** Easy
**Servings:** 2
**Preparation Time:** 15 minutes
**Cooking Time:** 15 minutes
**Ingredients:**
- ¼ c. all-purpose flour
- Salt, as required
- 3 (6-oz.) skinless, boneless chicken breast halves
- 2 tbsp. olive oil
- ¼ c. dry white wine
- 3 tbsp. freshly squeezed lime juice
- ¼ c. cold unsalted butter, cut into pieces
- 2 tbsp. capers, drained
- ½ lime, cut into wedges

**Directions:**
1. In a shallow dish, mix the flour and salt.
2. Add the chicken breasts and coat with flour mixture evenly.
3. Then, shake off the excess.

4. Heat the oil over medium-high heat in a cast-iron wok and cook the chicken breasts for about 3-4 minutes per side.

5. With a slotted spoon, transfer the chicken breasts onto a plate, and with a piece of foil, cover them to keep warm.

6. In the same wok, add the wine and bring to a boil, scraping up the browned bits from the bottom of the pan.

7. Add the lemon juice and cook for about 2-3 minutes or until reduced by half.

8. Add the butter and cook until the sauce becomes thick, shaking the pan vigorously.

9. Remove from the heat and stir in the capers.

10. Place the caper sauce over the chicken and serve with lime wedges.

**Nutrition (Per Serving):** Calories: 621 Fat: 43.3g Carbohydrates: 13.7g Fiber: 0.8g Sugar: 0.4g Protein: 40.1g

## 54.Chicken Marsala

❧*Don't stop when faced with difficulties. Everything becomes simple if you proceed in small steps*❧

**Difficulty Level:** Easy
**Servings:** 6
**Preparation Time:** 15 minutes
**Cooking Time:** 19 minutes
**Ingredients:**
- ¼ c. cake flour
- ½ tsp. dried oregano, crushed
- ½ tsp. salt
- ½ tsp. ground black pepper
- ¼ c. olive oil
- ½ c. butter

- 2½ lbs. chicken breasts
- 1 c. fresh mushrooms, sliced
- 1 medium onion, sliced
- ½ c. dry Marsala wine
- ¼ c. fresh parsley, chopped

**Directions:**
1. Add the flour, oregano, salt, and black pepper, and mix well in a bowl.

2. Coat the chicken breasts with flour mixture evenly and then shake off excess flour.

3. Heat oil and butter over medium heat in a large-sized cast-iron wok and cook the chicken breasts for about 2-3 minutes per side.

4. Now, arrange the mushroom and onion slices around the chicken breasts and cook for about 2 minutes without stirring.

5. Stir in the wine and cook, covered for about 10 minutes, stirring occasionally.

6. Serve hot with the garnishing of parsley.

**Nutrition (Per Serving):** Calories: 614 Fat: 07.9g Carbohydrates: 7g Fiber: 0.8g Sugar: 1.2g Protein: 56.1g

## 55.Ground Turkey with Lentils

❧*Clean the cast iron well by boiling the water with the salt inside and dry it thoroughly*❧
**Difficulty Level:** Easy
**Servings:** 8
**Preparation Time:** 15 minutes
**Cooking Time:** 35 minutes
**Ingredients:**
- 3 tbsp. olive oil, divided
- 1 onion, chopped
- 1 tbsp. fresh ginger, minced
- 4 garlic cloves, minced
- 2 Roma tomatoes, seeded and chopped
- 3 celery stalks, chopped
- 1 large carrot, peeled and chopped
- 1 c. dried red lentils, rinsed, soaked for 30 minutes, and drained
- 2 c. chicken broth
- 1 tsp. black mustard seeds
- 1½ tsp. cumin seeds
- 1 tsp. Ground turmeric
- ½ tsp. paprika
- 1 lb. lean ground turkey
- 1 Serrano pepper, seeded and chopped
- 2 scallions, chopped

**Directions:**

1. In a cast-iron saucepan, heat one tablespoon of oil over medium heat and sauté onion, ginger, and garlic for about 5 minutes. Stir in tomatoes, celery, carrot, lentils, and broth and bring to a boil

2. Reduce the heat to medium-low and simmer, covered for about 30 minutes. Meanwhile, heat the remaining oil in a cast-iron wok over medium heat and sauté mustard seeds and cumin seeds for about 30 seconds. Add turmeric and paprika and sauté for about 30 seconds.

3. Transfer the mixture into a small-sized bowl and set aside. Add turkey and cook for about 4-5 minutes in the same wok. Add Serrano pepper and scallion and cook for about 3-4 minutes.

4. Add spiced oil mixture and stir to combine well. Transfer the turkey mixture to simmering lentils and simmer for about 5-10 minutes more.

5. Serve hot.

**Nutrition (Per Serving):** Calories: 247 Fat: 10.3g Carbohydrates: 20.1g Fiber: 8.8g Sugar: 2.8g Protein: 19.5g

## 56. Taco Ground Turkey

*Gwenda loves using her cast iron wok when she wants to cook chicken*

**Difficulty Level:** Easy
**Servings:** 4
**Preparation Time:** 10 minutes
**Cooking Time:** 20 minutes
**Ingredients:**
- 1 tbsp. olive oil
- 1 lb. lean ground turkey
- 1 large yellow onion, chopped
- 3 c. fresh spinach
- 1 (14½-oz.) can of diced tomatoes with green chiles
- 2 tbsp. taco seasoning
- 1 tbsp. freshly squeezed lime juice
- 1½ c. Mexican cheese blend, shredded

**Directions:**

1. Heat the oil over medium heat in a large cast-iron wok and cook the ground turkey for about 6-8 minutes, breaking into small crumbles.

2. Add the onion over medium-low heat and cook for about 5-6 minutes, stirring occasionally.

3. Stir in the tomatoes and taco seasoning and cook for about 1-2 minutes.

4. Stir in the spinach and lime juice and cook for about 3-4 minutes.

5. Sprinkle with the cheese and immediately cover the wok.

6. Remove from the heat and set aside, covered for about 5 minutes before serving.

**Nutrition (Per Serving):** Calories: 259 Fat: 25.1g Carbohydrates: 12.8g Fiber: 2.5g Sugar: 5.1g Protein: 32.2g

## 57. Chicken with Cabbage

*Step by step the recipe is carried out even if it seems a bit difficult. The right mindset always works*

**Difficulty Level:** Hard
**Servings:** 4
**Preparation Time:** 15 minutes
**Cooking Time:** 20 minutes
**Ingredients:**
- 2 tbsp. olive oil, divided
- 3 garlic cloves, minced
- ½ of a large onion, chopped
- 1 lb. boneless, skinless chicken breasts, cut into bite-sized pieces
- ½ large green bell pepper, seeded and chopped
- 5 c. green cabbage, shredded
- ½ tsp. ground ginger
- ¼ c. low-sodium soy sauce
- Ground black pepper, as required
- 2 tbsp. fresh chives, chopped

**Directions:**

1. Heat one tablespoon of oil over medium heat in a large cast-iron wok and sauté the garlic for about 30 seconds. Add the onion and cook for about 5-7 minutes, stirring frequently.

2. Now, add the remaining oil over medium-high heat and stir fry the chicken pieces for about 3-5 minutes.

3. Stir in the bell pepper, cabbage, ground ginger, soy sauce, and black pepper, and stir fry for about 3-5 minutes.

4. Serve hot with the garnishing of chives.

**Nutrition (Per Serving):** Calories: 329 Fat: 15.6g Carbohydrates: 12g Fiber: 2.9g Sugar: 4.4g Protein: 34.4g

## 58. Roasted Chicken with Leeks

*❦Simple recipes are always the best then if cooked in cast iron even better❦*

**Difficulty Level:** Easy
**Servings:** 6
**Preparation Time:** 15 minutes
**Cooking Time:** 1 hour
**Ingredients:**

- 1 (4-lb.) whole chicken, neck, and giblets removed
- Salt, as required
- 3 leeks (white and pale green parts), halved lengthwise
- 3 tbsp. olive oil, divided
- Ground black pepper, as required

**Directions:**

1. Season the chicken with salt, inside and out generously.
2. With kitchen twine, tie the legs together. Set aside at room temperature for about 1 hour.
3. Preheat your oven to 425°F. Arrange a rack in the upper third of the oven.
4. Arrange a 12-inch cast-iron wok in a baking dish and place it into the oven to preheat.
5. Meanwhile, add leeks, two tablespoons of oil, salt, and black pepper in a bowl, and toss to coat well.
6. Dry the chicken and coat it with half of the remaining oil using paper towels.
7. Place the remaining oil in a hot wok and spread evenly.
8. Arrange the chicken in the center of the wok and place the leeks around it.
9. Roast for about 50-60 minutes.
10. Remove from the oven and set aside for about 5 minutes before carving.
11. Cut the chicken into desired-sized pieces with a sharp knife and serve.

**Nutrition (Per Serving):** Calories: 654 Fat: 44.9g
Carbohydrates: 6.3g Fiber: 0.8g Sugar: 1.7g Protein: 54.7g

## 59. Chicken with Pears

*❦Cooking with cast iron is always a great choice❦*

**Difficulty Level:** Medium
**Servings:** 4
**Preparation Time:** 15 minutes
**Cooking Time:** 25 minutes
**Ingredients:**

- 1 c. chicken broth
- 2 tbsp. apple cider vinegar
- 2 tsp. tapioca flour
- 2 tbsp. extra-virgin olive oil
- 4 garlic cloves, minced
- 2 tbsp. fresh basil, minced
- 4 (4-oz.) skinless, boneless chicken breasts
- Salt and ground black pepper, as required
- 2 Bosc pears, cored and sliced

**Directions:**

1. Blends together the broth, vinegar, and tapioca flour in a bowl. Set aside.
2. In a large-sized cast-iron wok, heat oil over medium-high heat and sauté garlic and basil for about 1 minute.
3. Add the chicken, salt, and black pepper and cook for about 12-15 minutes.
4. Transfer the chicken into a bowl.
5. Add the pears and cook for about 4-5 minutes in the same wok.
6. Add the broth mixture and bring to a boil.
7. Cook for about 1 minute.
8. Add the chicken and stir to combine.
9. Now adjust the heat to low and cook for about 3-4 minutes. Serve hot.

**Nutrition (Per Serving):** Calories: 284 Fat: 11.6g
Carbohydrates: 18.7g Fiber: 3.3g Sugar: 10.5g Protein: 27.1g

## 60. Chicken with Bell Peppers & Pineapple

*❧If you cook recipes with peppers it is important to clean the cast iron pan immediately to eliminate the strong odor❧*

**Difficulty Level:** Easy
**Servings:** 4
**Preparation Time:** 15 minutes
**Cooking Time:** 20 minutes
**Ingredients:**
- 1 tbsp. extra-virgin olive oil
- 1 large onion, chopped
- 1 garlic clove, minced
- 1 tsp. fresh ginger, minced
- 2 skinless, boneless chicken breasts, cubed
- 2 c. fresh pineapple, cubed
- 2 tomatoes, seeded and chopped
- 1 medium red bell pepper, seeded and chopped
- 1 medium green bell pepper, seeded and chopped
- 1 medium orange bell pepper, seeded and chopped
- 2 tbsp. soy sauce
- 1 tbsp. apple cider vinegar
- Ground black pepper, as required

**Directions:**
1. Heat the oil over medium heat in a large cast-iron wok and sauté the onion for about 4-5 minutes.
2. Add the garlic and ginger and sauté for about 1 minute.
3. Add the chicken and cook for about 4-5 minutes or until browned from all sides.
4. Add the pineapple, tomatoes, and bell peppers and cook for about 5-6 minutes or until vegetables become tender.
5. Add the soy sauce, vinegar, and black pepper and cook for about 2-3 minutes.
6. Serve hot.

**Nutrition (Per Serving):** Calories: 296 Fat: 10.3g Carbohydrates: 24.6g Fiber: 4.1g Sugar: 16g Protein: 27.9g

## 61. Ground Turkey & Pasta Stew

*❧Cast iron is very versatile, you can cook many different dishes❧*

**Difficulty Level:** Easy
**Servings:** 8
**Preparation Time:** 15 minutes
**Cooking Time:** 40 minutes

**Ingredients:**
- 1½ lbs. lean ground turkey
- 1 carrot, peeled and chopped
- 1 celery stalk, chopped
- 1 c. tomato sauce
- 1 (14-oz.) can stewed, chopped tomatoes
- 2 tsp. white sugar
- 3 garlic cloves, minced
- ½ tsp. dried basil, crushed
- 1 (16-oz.) package of dried pasta (of your choice)

**Directions:**
1. Heat a large-sized cast-iron saucepan over medium heat and cook turkey for about 8-10 minutes or until browned.
2. Stir in the carrot, celery, tomato sauce, tomatoes, sugar, garlic cloves, and basil and bring to a gentle boil
3. Now adjust the heat to low and simmer for about 20 minutes.
4. Meanwhile, add pasta and cook for about 8-10 minutes in a large-sized saucepan of salted boiling water.
5. Drain the pasta well.
6. Add pasta into the pan with turkey mixture and cook for about 4-5 minutes.
7. Serve hot.

**Nutrition (Per Serving):** Calories: 310 Fat: 7.6g Carbohydrates: 36.8g Fiber: 1.3g Sugar: 4g Protein: 21.4g

## 62. Chicken Parmigiana

*❧The "seasoning" of the cast iron is obtained with a long cooking of a layer of fat inside the pan. The fat will create a protective, non-stick layer❧*

**Difficulty Level:** Hard
**Servings:** 4
**Preparation Time:** 15 minutes
**Cooking Time:** 30 minutes
**Ingredients:**

- 16 oz. frozen grilled chicken breast strips
- 1 (14½-oz.) can diced tomatoes with juice
- (6-oz.) can tomato paste
- 2 tbsp. dry red wine
- 1 tbsp. olive oil
- 1½ tsp. Italian seasoning
- 1 garlic clove, minced
- ½ tsp, white sugar
- ⅓ c. Parmesan cheese, shredded
- ⅓ c. part-skim mozzarella cheese, shredded

**Directions:**

1. Heat a lightly greases cast-iron wok over medium heat and cook the chicken strips for about 5-8 minutes or until heated through.
2. With a slotted spoon, transfer the chicken strips onto a plate.
3. In the same wok, add the remaining ingredients except for cheese and bring to a boil, stirring occasionally.
4. Adjust the heat to low and simmer, uncovered for about 10-15 minutes, stirring occasionally.
5. Stir in chicken strips and sprinkle with both cheeses.
6. Cover the wok and cook for about 1-2 minutes or until cheese is melted.

7. Serve hot.

**Nutrition (Per Serving):** Calories: 321 Fat: 11.3g
Carbohydrates: 15.2g Fiber: 3.5g Sugar: 9.8g
Protein: 38.9g

## 63. Chicken Madeira

*❧Practice makes you an Expert❧*
**Difficulty Level:** Easy
**Servings:** 4
**Preparation Time:** 15 minutes
**Cooking Time:** 40 minutes
**Ingredients:**

- 4 (5-oz.) boneless, skinless chicken breasts
- Salt and ground black pepper, as required
- 4 tbsp. butter, divided
- 2 c. fresh mushrooms, sliced
- 2 c. beef broth
- 2 c. Madeira wine
- ½ lb. asparagus, trimmed
- 4 oz. mozzarella cheese
- ¼ c. Parmesan cheese, shredded

**Directions:**

1. With a meat mallet, lb., each chicken breast slightly. Season each chicken breast with salt and black pepper evenly.
2. In a large wok, melt two tablespoons of butter over medium-high heat and cook the chicken breasts for about 4-5 minutes per side.
3. With a slotted spoon, transfer the chicken breasts onto a plate. In the same wok, add remaining butter and mushroom over medium-high heat and cook for about 2 minutes, without stirring.
4. Stir the mushrooms and cook for about 3-4 minutes, stirring frequently.
5. Transfer the mushrooms onto the plate with the chicken with the slotted spoon.
6. In the same wok, add the broth and wine and bring to a boil, scraping up the browned bits from the bottom of the pan.
7. Adjust the heat to low and simmer for about 10-12 minutes. Meanwhile, cook the asparagus for about 3-5 minutes in a pan of boiling water.
8. In the wok with wine sauce, stir in the cooked chicken, mushrooms, and asparagus and cook for about 1-2 minutes.

9. Sprinkle the Mozzarella cheese on top and cook, covered for about 2-3 minutes or until cheese is melted. Serve hot with the garnishing of Parmesan cheese.

**Nutrition (Per Serving):** Calories: 610 Fat: 29.2g Carbohydrates: 8.1g Fiber: 1.5g Sugar: 2.8g Protein: 55.9g

8. Slowly, add the arrowroot starch mixture, stirring continuously. Cook for about 3-4 minutes or until desired thickness, stirring occasionally. Serve hot with the topping of chopped dill.

**Nutrition (Per Serving):** Calories: 514 Fat: 22.5g Carbohydrates: 4.6g Fiber: 0.5g Sugar: 1g Protein: 69.2g

## 64. Chicken Thighs in Dill Sauce

*⚜The unmistakable aroma of chopped fresh dill makes this dish pleasant and tasty⚜*

**Difficulty Level:** Easy
**Servings:** 6
**Preparation Time:** 10 minutes
**Cooking Time:** 1 hour 5 minutes
**Ingredients:**
- 6 (8-oz.) bone-in chicken thighs
- Salt and ground black pepper, as required
- 2 tbsp. olive oil
- ½ of onion, slice
- 4 c. chicken broth
- ½ tsp. ground turmeric
- 8 sprigs of fresh dill
- 2 tbsp. freshly squeezed lemon juice
- 2 tbsp. arrowroot starch
- 1 tbsp. water
- ½ tbsp. fresh dill, chopped

**Directions:**
1. Sprinkle the chicken thighs with salt and black pepper. In a large-sized cast-iron wok, heat the olive oil over high heat.
2. Place the chicken thighs in wok, skin side down, and cook for about 3-4 minutes per side.
3. With a slotted spoon, transfer the thighs onto a plate. Add onion over medium heat and sauté for about 4-5 minutes in the same wok.
4. Return the thighs in wok, skin side up with broth, turmeric, salt, and black pepper.
5. Place the dill sprigs and over thighs and bring to a boil. Adjust the heat to medium-low and simmer, covered for about 40-45 minutes, coating the thighs with cooking liquid.
6. Meanwhile, in a small-sized bowl, mix arrowroot starch and water.
7. Discard the thyme sprigs and transfer the thighs into a bowl. Add the lemon juice in sauce and stir to combine.

## 65. Ground Turkey & Potato Soup

*⚜Cast iron is composed of iron and carbon, it is very resistant and does not get damaged⚜*

**Difficulty Level:** Hard
**Servings:** 8
**Preparation Time:** 15 minutes
**Cooking Time:** 45 minutes
**Ingredients:**
- 2 tbsp. olive oil
- 1 yellow onion, chopped
- 2 c. carrots, peeled and chopped
- 2 celery stalks, chopped
- 2 garlic cloves, minced
- 1½ lbs. lean ground turkey
- 4 c. tomatoes, crushed finely
- 2 tsp. red chili powder
- 3½ c. potatoes, cubed
- 2 c. sweet potato, peeled and cubed
- 8 c. low-sodium chicken broth
- Salt and ground black pepper, as required

**Directions:**
1. In a large-sized cast-iron saucepan, heat the olive oil over medium heat and sauté the onions and carrots for about 3 minutes.
2. Add the garlic and sauté for about 1 minute.
3. Add ground turkey and cook for about 7-8 minutes, breaking up the chunks with a wooden spoon.
4. Add tomatoes and chili powder and cook for about four more minutes.
5. Add the potatoes and broth and bring to a boil.
6. Adjust the heat to low and cook, covered for about 20-25 minutes, stirring occasionally.
7. Stir in the salt and black pepper and serve hot.

**Nutrition (Per Serving):** Calories: 294 Fat: 10.1g Carbohydrates: 29.9g Fiber: 5.6g Sugar: 8.4g Protein: 22.1g

## 66.Creamy Chicken & Spinach

❧*The result of cooking in cast iron does not disappoint anyone*❧

**Difficulty Level:** Easy
**Servings:** 4
**Preparation Time:** 15 minutes
**Cooking Time:** 20 minutes
**Ingredients:**
- 2 tbsp. butter, divided
- 4 (4-oz.) boneless, skinless chicken thighs
- Salt and ground black pepper, as required
- 2 garlic cloves, minced
- 1 jalapeño pepper, chopped
- 10 oz. frozen spinach, thawed
- ¼ c. Parmesan cheese, shredded
- ¼ c. heavy cream

**Directions:**
1. In a large-sized cast-iron wok, melt one tablespoon of the butter over medium-high heat and cook the chicken with salt and black pepper for about 5-6 minutes per side.
2. Transfer the chicken into a bowl.
3. In the same wok, melt the remaining butter over medium-low heat and sauté the garlic for about 1 minute.
4. Add the spinach and cook for about 1 minute.
5. Add the cheese, cream, salt, and black pepper and stir to combine.
6. Spread the spinach mixture in the bottom of the wok evenly.
7. Place chicken over spinach in a single layer.
8. Immediately adjust the heat to low and cook, covered for about 5 minutes.
9. Serve hot.
**Nutrition (Per Serving):** Calories: 395Fat: 22.7g Carbohydrates: 4.2g Fiber: 1.7g Sugar: 0.5g Protein: 42.8g

## 67.Turkey Breast with Mustard Sauce

❧*The combination of the ingredients in this recipe creates a truly exquisite dish*❧

**Difficulty Level:** Medium
**Servings:** 4
**Preparation Time:** 10 minutes
**Cooking Time:** 20 minutes
**Ingredients:**
- 1 (2-lb.) boneless, skinless turkey breast half
- Salt and ground black pepper, as required
- 2 tbsp. olive oil
- 2 c. dry white wine
- ¼ c. Dijon mustard
- ¼ c. fresh parsley, chopped

**Directions:**
1. With plastic wrap, cover the turkey breast and, with a meat mallet, lb. it lightly.
2. Slice the turkey breast into equal-sized eight cutlets.
3. Season the turkey cutlets with salt and black pepper.
4. In a large-sized cast-iron wok, heat oil over high heat and cook the turkey cutlets for about 3-4 minutes per side.
5. With a slotted spoon, transfer the turkey cutlets onto a plate, and cover them loosely with a piece of foil.
6. Add wine into the wok and bring to a boil.
7. Cook for about 6-8 minutes, scraping up the browned bits with a wooden spoon.
8. Stir in the mustard and bring to a gentle simmer.

9.      Remove from heat and stir in the parsley, salt, and black pepper.

10.     Pour the sauce over turkey cutlets and serve.

**Nutrition (Per Serving):** Calories: 390Fat: 8.7g Carbohydrates: 4.3g Fiber: 0.6g Sugar: 1.1g Protein: 57.1g

## 68. Ground Turkey in Marinara Sauce

*⚜Only true connoisseurs understand the value of a dish cooked in cast iron⚜*

**Difficulty Level:** Easy
**Servings:** 3
**Preparation Time:** 10 minutes
**Cooking Time:** 22 minutes
**Ingredients:**
- 1 tbsp. extra-virgin olive oil
- 1 large onion, chopped
- 1 lb. ground turkey
- 2 garlic cloves, minced
- 1 tbsp. dried oregano
- 1 tsp. red pepper flakes, crushed
- 2 c. marinara sauce
- 2 tbsp. fresh parsley, chopped

**Directions:**
1.      In a large-sized cast-iron wok, heat the oil over medium heat and sauté the onion for about 5 minutes.

2.      Add the ground turkey, garlic, oregano, and red pepper flakes and cook for about 6-7 minutes.

3.      Stir in the marinara sauce and simmer for about 8-10 minutes.

4.      Serve hot with the garnishing of parsley.

**Nutrition (Per Serving):** Calories: 328 Fat: 18.8g Carbohydrates: 11.5g Fiber: 2.7g Sugar: 5.6g Protein: 28.1g

## 69. Turkey & Pumpkin Stew

*⚜If you love pumpkin stew and turkey try this recipe at least once⚜*

**Difficulty Level:** Easy
**Servings:** 6
**Preparation Time:** 15 minutes
**Cooking Time:** 50 minutes
**Ingredients:**
- 2 tbsp. canola oil, divided

- 4 large scallions, chopped
- 2 tsp. ginger, grated finely
- 24 oz. cooked boneless turkey cutlet, chopped
- 1 c. pumpkin puree
- 1 (14-oz.) can crushed tomatoes
- 1 c. water
- 1 tsp. white sugar
- Salt and ground black pepper, as required
- ¼ c. fresh cilantro, chopped

**Directions:**
1.      In a large-sized cast-iron saucepan, heat one tablespoon of oil over medium heat and sauté scallion for about 2minutes.

2.      Add ginger and sauté for about 2 minutes.

3.      Transfer the scallion mixture into a bowl.

4.      Heat the remaining oil over medium heat in the same pan and cook turkey for about 3-4 minutes.

5.      Stir in scallion mixture and remaining ingredients except for cilantro and bring to a boil.

6.      Reduce the heat to low and cook, partially covered for about 40 minutes.

7.      Stir in cilantro and simmer for about 2 minutes.

8.      Serve hot.

**Nutrition (Per Serving):** Calories: 284 Fat: 10.5g Carbohydrates: 10.9g Fiber: 3.8g Sugar: 6.1g Protein: 35.6g

## 70. Ground Turkey, Beans & Corn Chili

*⚜Cast iron is very resistant but should never be washed in the dishwasher⚜*

**Difficulty Level:** Easy
**Servings:** 6
**Preparation Time:** 15 minutes
**Cooking Time:** 45 minutes
**Ingredients:**
- 2 tbsp. olive oil
- 1 red bell pepper, seeded and chopped
- 1 onion, chopped
- 2 garlic cloves, chopped
- 1 lb. lean ground turkey
- 2 c. water
- 3 c. tomatoes, chopped finely
- 1 tsp. ground cumin

- ½ tsp. ground cinnamon
- 1 (15-oz.) can of red kidney beans, rinsed and drained
- 1½ c, frozen corn, thawed
- ¼ c. scallion greens, chopped

**Directions:**

1. Heat the olive oil over medium-low heat and sauté bell pepper, onion, and garlic for about 5 minutes in a large-sized cast-iron saucepan.
2. Add turkey and cook for about 5-6 minutes, breaking up the chunks with a wooden spoon.
3. Add water, tomatoes, and spices and bring to a boil over high heat.
4. Adjust the heat to medium-low and stir in beans and corn.
5. Simmer, covered for about 30 minutes, stirring occasionally.
6. Serve hot with the topping of scallion greens.

**Nutrition (Per Serving):** Calories: 270 Fat: 10.9g Carbohydrates: 27g Fiber: 6.9g Sugar: 7.2g Protein: 21.3g

# CHAPTER 4:

# Fish And Seafood Recipes

## 71. Sardines with Hearts of Palm

*❧Cook any dish in cast iron and you will get excellent results❧*

**Difficulty Level:** Easy
**Servings:** 4
**Preparation Time:** 10 minutes
**Cooking Time:** 36 minutes
**Ingredients:**
- ½ lb. fingerling potatoes halved lengthwise
- 1 small sweet onion, coarsely chopped
- 2 garlic cloves, thickly sliced
- ¼ tsp. red pepper flakes, or to taste
- 3 tbsp. extra-virgin olive oil
- Salt, to taste
- ⅓ c. oil-packed, sun-dried tomatoes, drained and coarsely chopped
- ½ lemon, very thinly sliced and seeded
- 1 (14-oz.) can hearts of palm, drained and cut into bite-size pieces
- 1 (5-oz.) can oil-packed smoked sardines, drained

**Directions:**
1. Preheat the oven to 450°F.
2. Combine the first six ingredients (through salt) in a large bowl, tossing to coat with oil and salt.
3. Spread mixture over bottom of cast iron skillet. Keep any remaining oil in the bowl.
4. To the same bowl, add sun-dried tomatoes and lemon slices. Toss to coat with oil from the bowl.
5. Place tomato and lemon slices over potato mixture.
6. Bake until potatoes are tender (about 25 minutes).
7. Add hearts of palm and bake 5 minutes longer.
8. Add sardines and bake to heat through (1 minute).
9. Serve immediately.

**Nutrition (Per Serving):** Calories: 457 Fat: 26.4 g Carbohydrates: 34.2 g Protein: 23.4 g Sodium: 1466 mg

## 72. Stuffed Salmon

**Difficulty Level:** Medium
**Servings:** 4
**Preparation Time:** 15 minutes
**Cooking Time:** 16 minutes
**Ingredients:**
For the Salmon:
- 4 (6-oz.) skinless salmon fillets
- Salt and ground black pepper, as required
- 2 tbsp. freshly squeezed lemon juice
- 2 tbsp. olive oil, divided
- 1 tbsp. unsalted butter
For the Filling:
- 4 oz. cream cheese, softened
- ¼ c. Parmesan cheese, grated finely
- 4 oz. frozen spinach, thawed and squeezed
- 2 tsp. garlic, minced
- Salt and ground black pepper, as required

**Directions:**
1. Season each salmon fillet with salt and black pepper, and then drizzle with lemon juice and one tablespoon of oil.
2. Arrange the salmon fillets onto a smooth surface.
3. With a sharp knife, cut a pocket into each salmon fillet about ¾ of the way through, being careful not to cut all the way.
For the Filling:
1. Add the cream cheese, Parmesan cheese, spinach, garlic, salt, and black pepper in a bowl and mix well.
2. Place about 1-2 tablespoons of spinach mixture into each salmon pocket and spread evenly.
3. Heat the remaining oil and butter over medium-high heat in a cast-iron wok and cook the salmon fillets for about 6-8 minutes per side.
4. Remove the salmon fillets from heat and transfer them onto the serving plates.
5. Serve immediately.

**Nutrition (Per Serving):** Calories: 440 Fat: 32g Carbohydrates: 2.4g Fiber: 0.7g Sugar: 0.4g Protein: 38.1g

## 73. Shrimp Casserole

⚜ ⚜ ⚜

**Difficulty Level:** Easy
**Servings:** 2
**Preparation Time:** 10 minutes
**Cooking Time:** 35 minutes
**Ingredients:**
- ½ lb. medium shrimp
- Shells from shrimp
- 1 c. heavy cream
- 1 tbsp. sherry
- Salt, to taste
- 2 tbsp. unsalted butter, divided
- 1 c. small oyster crackers, broken into coarse crumbs
- ⅛ tsp. sweet paprika
- 2 medium scallions, white and tender green parts, minced
- ½ tsp. fresh lemon juice
- 1 tsp. Worcestershire sauce
- Freshly ground pepper, to taste
- Hot sauce, to taste (optional)

**Directions:**
1. Clean and devein shrimp. Set aside shells for making sauce. Cover shrimp and refrigerate until ready to cook. Place shells, cream, sherry, and salt in a small saucepan. Simmer gently over low heat to infuse flavor (about 8–10 minutes). Strain out shells. Set aside sauce.
2. Preheat oven to 400°F. Melt butter in a skillet over medium heat. Scoop out one tablespoon and mix with crumbs and paprika. Set aside.
3. Add scallions to skillet and cook until softened (about 3 minutes). Add cream-sherry mixture and reduce heat to low. Simmer until reduced (about 3 minutes). Remove from heat. Stir in lemon juice and Worcestershire sauce. Season with salt, pepper, and hot sauce according to taste. Let sauce cool to lukewarm while seasoning the shrimp with salt and pepper.
4. Place shrimp into skillet and toss to coat well with the sauce. Top with crumbs and place on the middle rack in the oven. Bake until bubbling at edges and shrimp is cooked through (about 15–20 minutes).
5. Remove from oven. Preheat broiler. Place under broiler until crumbs are browned (about 30 seconds). Let stand for 5 minutes before serving.
**Nutrition (Per Serving):** Calories: 679, Fat: 58 g Carbohydrates: 10.3 g Protein: 26 g Sodium: 595 mg

## 74. Seared Stuffed Trout

⚜ ⚜ ⚜

**Difficulty Level:** Easy
**Servings:** 2
**Preparation Time:** 20 minutes
**Cooking Time:** 8–10 minutes
**Ingredients:**
- 1 c. packed escarole, chopped (other options: arugula, spinach, or mustard greens)
- 1 small shallot, thinly sliced
- ½ tsp. lemon juice
- 1 tsp. extra-virgin olive oil
- Salt and freshly ground pepper, to taste
- 2 pieces of the whole trout, about 12 oz. each, cleaned
- 1 tbsp. cornmeal or flour, for sprinkling
- Oil, for frying
- 2 tbsp. unsalted butter
- Lemon wedges, for serving

**Directions:**
1. Toss escarole, shallot, lemon juice, olive oil, salt, and pepper together in a bowl.
2. Stuff trout with escarole mixture and seal with skewers.
3. Season with salt and pepper.
4. Sprinkle lightly and evenly with cornmeal.
5. Heat oil, about ⅛-inch deep, in a cast-iron skillet over medium heat.
6. Cook fish until skin is crisp and inside is cooked through (about 8–10 minutes). Remove from skillet.
7. Wipe a skillet or use a new skillet to melt butter over medium heat.
8. Place trout in skillet and coat evenly with melted butter. Remove from heat and let fish rest in skillet for 5 minutes.
9. Serve with lemon wedges.
**Nutrition (Per Serving):** Calories: 558 Fat: 30.4 g
Carbohydrates: 2.5 g Protein: 65.6 g Sodium: 458 mg

## 75.Seafood Skillet Roast

⚜ ⚜ ⚜

**Difficulty Level:** Easy
**Servings:** 2
**Preparation Time:** 10 minutes
**Cooking Time:** 6–8 minutes
**Ingredients**:
- 1 small shallot, minced
- ¼ fennel bulb, minced
- 1 tbsp. fennel frond, finely chopped
- 2 jumbo shrimp, butterflied in their shells
- 2 (8-oz.) South African lobster tails, halved lengthwise
- 2 oysters, shucked and both shells reserved
- 2 large scallops
- Garlic toast, for serving

For the Vinaigrette:
- 3 tbsp. fresh lemon juice
- 2 tbsp. crème fraîche
- 5 tbsp. extra-virgin olive oil
- Salt and pepper, to taste

**Directions:**
1. If using frozen seafood, thaw thoroughly and pat dry with paper towels.
2. Whisk the vinaigrette ingredients in a medium bowl.
3. Stir in shallot, a fennel bulb, and a fennel frond.
4. Preheat broiler and position rack 6 inches underneath.
5. Arrange the seafood in a single layer in a cast-iron skillet, placing scallops on top of extra oyster shells.
6. Spoon about half of the vinaigrette over seafood, coating evenly, and season with salt and pepper.
7. Broil until lightly browned (about 6–8 minutes).
8. Drizzle with remaining vinaigrette and serve with garlic toast.

**Nutrition (Per Serving):** Calories: 635 Fat: 48.8 g Carbohydrates: 22.5 g Protein: 22.8 g Sodium: 1252 mg

## 76.Seasoned Tilapia

⚜ ⚜ ⚜

**Difficulty Level:** Easy
**Servings:** 4
**Preparation Time:** 10 minutes
**Cooking Time:** 8 minutes
**Ingredients:**
- 4 (5-oz.) tilapia fillets
- 2 tbsp. BBQ seasoning
- Salt and ground black pepper, as required
- 2 tsp. olive oil

**Directions:**
1. Season each tilapia fillet with BBQ seasoning, salt, and black pepper.
2. In a cast-iron saucepan, heat oil over medium-high heat and cook the tilapia fillets for about 3-4 minutes per side or until cooked through.
3. Divide tilapia fillets onto serving plates.
4. Serve hot.

**Nutrition (Per Serving):** Calories: 142 Fat: 3.7g Carbohydrates: 0.7g Fiber: 0.2g Sugar: 0.2g Protein: 26.8g

## 77.Lemony Cod with Capers

⚜*There are many types of cast iron skillets and pots, and almost all formats fit any recipe*⚜

**Difficulty Level:** Easy
**Servings:** 2
**Preparation Time:** 15 minutes
**Cooking Time:** 7–10 minutes
**Ingredients:**
- 8–12 oz. skinless cod fillets
- Salt and pepper, to taste
- 2 tbsp. all-purpose flour
- 2 tbsp. olive oil

- Juice of 1 small lemon
- 2 tbsp. unsalted butter
- 2 cloves of smashed garlic
- 2 tbsp. capers, drained
- Fresh parsley leaves, chopped, for garnish

**Directions:**

1. Thaw fillets, if frozen, and pat dry with paper towels.
2. Season with salt and pepper, and then sprinkle evenly with flour.
3. Heat oil in a skillet over medium heat.
4. Cook fillets until golden brown and cooked through (about 3 minutes on each side).
5. Transfer to a plate and tent loosely with aluminum foil.
6. Add lemon juice to skillet and bring to a boil.
7. Add the butter, garlic, and capers.
8. Cook until fragrant (about 1 minute).
9. Drizzle over fish.
10. Sprinkle with parsley and serve.

**Nutrition (Per Serving):** Calories: 253 Fat: 16.3 g Carbohydrates: 5.5 g Protein: 21.2 g Sodium: 348 mg

## 78. Salmon with Couscous

❧ ❧ ❧

**Difficulty Level:** Easy
**Servings:** 4
**Preparation Time:** 20 minutes
**Cooking Time:** 22 minutes
**Ingredients:**

- 1¼ lbs. boneless, skinless salmon, cut into four equal-sized portions
- Salt and ground black pepper as required
- 4 tbsp. sun-dried tomato pesto, divided
- 2 tbsp. extra-virgin olive oil, divided
- 2 medium fennel bulbs, cut into ½-inch wedges and fronds reserved
- 1 c. whole-wheat couscous
- 3 scallions, sliced thinly
- ¼ c. green olives, pitted and sliced
- 2 tbsp. pine nuts, toasted
- 2 garlic cloves, sliced
- 2 tsp. lemon zest, grated finely
- 1½ c. low-sodium chicken broth
- 1 lemon, cut into eight slices

**Directions:**

1. Season the salmon prices with salt and black pepper evenly. Then, spread 1½ teaspoon of the pesto on each salmon piece evenly. In a large cast-iron wok, heat one tablespoon of the oil over medium-high heat and cook half of the fennel for about 2-3 minutes or until brown on the bottom. With a slotted spoon, transfer the fennel onto a plate. Repeat with the remaining oil and fennel.
2. In the same wok, add the couscous and scallions over medium heat and cook for about 1-2 minutes or lightly toasted, stirring frequently.
3. Add the olives, pine nuts, garlic, lemon zest, remaining two tablespoons of the pesto, and broth and stir to combine. Place the cooked fennel and salmon on top and gently press into the couscous mixture. Arrange the lemon slices on top evenly.
4. Reduce the heat to medium-low and cook, covered for about 10-14 minutes or until the desired doneness of the salmon and couscous.
5. Remove from the heat and serve hot with the topping of reserved fennel fronds.

**Nutrition (Per Serving):** Calories: 594 Fat: 29.3g Carbohydrates: 47.7g Fiber: 7.7g Sugar: 1.5g Protein: 37.9g

## 79. Spicy Shrimp with White Beans and Tomatoes

❧ ❧ ❧

**Difficulty Level:** Hard
**Servings:** 2
**Preparation Time:** 5 minutes
**Cooking Time:** 8–10 minutes
**Ingredients:**

- 2 tbsp. olive oil
- 1½ c. cherry tomatoes halved
- 2 cloves garlic, minced
- ¼ tsp. red pepper flakes, or to taste
- ⅓ c. dry white wine
- 1 (15-oz.) can white beans, drained and rinsed
- Kosher salt, to taste
- ½ lb. uncooked medium shrimp, peeled and deveined
- 2 tbsp. fresh parsley leaves, coarsely chopped

**Directions:**

1.	Heat oil in a cast-iron skillet over medium heat.

2.	Sauté tomatoes until softened (about 2 minutes).

3.	Add garlic and red pepper flakes and cook until fragrant (about 30 seconds).

4.	Add wine and cook until reduced (about 1 minute).

5.	Stir in beans and season with salt.

6.	Add shrimp and reduce heat to low.

7.	Cover and let cook until shrimp are opaque (about 3–4 minutes).

8.	Sprinkle with parsley and serve immediately.

**Nutrition (Per Serving):** Calories: 404 Fat: 8.8 g Carbohydrates: 50.7 g Protein: 31.9 g Sodium: 992 mg

## 80.Spicy Salmon

⚜ ⚜ ⚜

**Difficulty Level:** Easy
**Servings:** 4
**Preparation Time:** 10 minutes
**Cooking Time:** 8 minutes
**Ingredients:**

- 2 tsp. ground cumin
- 2 tsp. red chili powder
- 2 tsp. paprika
- 2 tsp. garlic powder
- Salt and ground black pepper, as required
- 4 (6-oz.) skinless salmon fillets
- 2 tbsp. butter

**Directions:**

1.	In a small-sized bowl, mix the spices.

2.	Coat the salmon fillets with the spice mixture evenly.

3.	Melt butter over medium-high heat and cook salmon fillets for about 3 minutes in a cast-iron wok.

4.	Flip and cook for about 4-5 minutes or until desired doneness.

5.	Serve hot.

**Nutrition (Per Serving):** Calories: 292 Fat: 16.9g Carbohydrates: 2.8g Fiber: 1.1g Sugar: 0.6g Protein: 33.8g

## 81.Zesty Salmon

⚜ ⚜ ⚜

**Difficulty Level:** Easy
**Servings:** 4
**Preparation Time:** 10 minutes
**Cooking Time:** 10 minutes
**Ingredients:**

- 2 tbsp. scallions, chopped
- ¾ tsp. fresh ginger, minced
- 1 garlic clove, minced
- ½ tsp. dried dill weed, crushed
- ¼ c. olive oil
- 2 tbsp. balsamic vinegar
- 2 tbsp. low-sodium soy sauce
- 4 (5-oz.) boneless salmon fillets

**Directions:**

1.	Add all ingredients except for salmon in a large-sized bowl and mix well. Add salmon and coat with marinade generously.

2.	Cover and refrigerate to marinate for at least 4-5 hours. Preheat a greased cast-iron grill pan over medium heat and cook the salmon fillets for about 5 minutes per side.

3.	Serve hot.

**Nutrition (Per Serving):** Calories: 303 Fat: 21.4g Carbohydrates: 1.4g Fiber: 0.2g Sugar: 0.4g Protein: 28.2g

## 82.Lemony Trout

⚜ ⚜ ⚜

**Difficulty Level:** Easy
**Servings:** 2
**Preparation Time:** 10 minutes
**Cooking Time:** 5 minutes
**Ingredients:**

- 2 (6-oz.) skin-on trout fillets

- Salt and ground black pepper, as required
- 4 tbsp. butter
- 4 fresh thyme sprigs
- 1 small lemon, sliced thinly
- 2 tbsp. freshly squeezed lemon juice
- 1 tbsp. fresh parsley, chopped

**Directions:**

1. Season the trout fillets with salt and black pepper evenly.
2. In a large-sized cast-iron wok, melt the butter over medium-high heat.
3. Place the trout fillets, skin side down, in the wok.
4. Place the thyme sprigs and lemon slices over fillets evenly.
5. Cook for about 5 minutes, pour the butter over fillets occasionally.
6. Transfer the trout fillets and lemon slices onto serving plates with a slotted spoon.
7. Remove the wok from the heat and stir in the lemon juice.
8. Place the pan sauce over the fillets and serve with the garnishing of parsley.

**Nutrition (Per Serving):** Calories: 533 Fat: 37.6g Carbohydrates: 0.8g Fiber: 0.3g Sugar: 0.4g Protein: 45.4g

## 83. Halibut with Leeks and Carrots

*⚜1 of the many qualities of the cast iron skillet is its ability to retain heat for a long time⚜*

**Difficulty Level:** Easy
**Servings:** 2
**Preparation Time:** 5 minutes
**Cooking Time:** 27–30 minutes
**Ingredients:**

- 3 tbsp. extra-virgin olive oil
- ½ lb. baby carrots
- ½ c. water, plus a little more if needed
- 3 medium leeks sliced crosswise
- Salt, to taste
- White pepper, to taste
- 3 sprigs thyme
- 1 bay leaf
- 2 skinless halibut fillets, about 1 inch thick

**Directions:**

1. Preheat the oven to 375°F.
2. Heat two tablespoons of oil in a cast-iron skillet over medium-high heat.

3. Stir-fry carrots until lightly golden (about 3 minutes).
4. Add water, cover, and continue cooking until carrots are crisp-tender (about 3–5 minutes).
5. Add leeks (and a little more water, if needed), cover, and cook until soft (about 5 minutes).
6. Season with salt and pepper.
7. Add thyme and bay leaf.
8. Sprinkle salt and white pepper over fish and lay on top of vegetables.
9. Drizzle fish with remaining oil.
10. Top with parchment paper and cover with a tight-fitting lid.
11. Place in oven and bake until fish is cooked through (about 15 minutes).
12. Discards herbs and serve.

**Nutrition (Per Serving):** Calories: 457 Fat: 22 g Carbohydrates: 26 g Protein: 42 g

## 84. Herb Crusted Salmon

**Difficulty Level:** Easy
**Servings:** 4
**Preparation Time:** 15 minutes
**Cooking Time:** 13 minutes
**Ingredients:**

- ¾ tsp. lemon-pepper seasoning
- 1 tsp. dried thyme
- 1 tsp. dried parsley
- 4 (5-oz.) salmon fillets
- 5 tbsp. freshly squeezed lemon juice, divided
- 10 tbsp. butter, divided
- 1 shallot, minced
- 5 tbsp. white wine, divided
- 1 tbsp. white wine vinegar
- 1 c. half-and-half
- Salt and ground white pepper, as required

**Directions:**

1. Mix the lemon pepper seasoning and dried herbs in a small-sized bowl.
2. In a shallow dish, place the salmon filets and rub them with three tablespoons of lemon juice.

3.    Season the non-skin side with herb mixture. Set aside. In a cast-iron wok, melt two tablespoons of butter over medium heat, and sauté the shallot for about 2 minutes.

4.    Stir in the remaining lemon juice, ¼ c. of wine, and vinegar, and simmer for about 2-3 minutes. Stir in half-and-half salt and white pepper and cook for about 2-3 minutes.

5.    Add four tablespoons of butter and beat until well combined.

6.    Remove from the heat and set aside, covered to keep warm. In a cast-iron wok, melt the remaining butter over medium heat.

7.    Place salmon in the wok, herb side down, and cook for about 1-2 minutes.

8.    Transfer the salmon fillets onto a plate, herb side up. In the wok, add the remaining wine, scraping up the browned bits from the bottom.

9.    Place the salmon fillets into the wok, herb side up, and cook for about 8 minutes.

10.    Transfer the salmon fillets onto serving plates. Top with pan sauce and serve.

**Nutrition (Per Serving):** Calories: 546 Fat: 44.7g Carbohydrates: 4.6g Fiber: 0.3g Sugar: 0.7g Protein: 29.9g

## 85.Honey Mustard Salmon

❀ ❀ ❀

**Difficulty Level:** Easy
**Servings:** 4
**Preparation Time:** 10 minutes
**Cooking Time:** 8 minutes
**Ingredients:**
- 1 (1-inch) piece of fresh ginger, grated finely
- 1 tbsp. honey
- 1 tbsp. freshly squeezed lemon juice
- 1 tbsp. Dijon mustard
- 2 tbsp. olive oil
- 4 (6-oz.) salmon fillets
- 2 tbsp. fresh parsley, chopped

**Directions:**
1.    Mix ginger, honey, lemon juice, and mustard in a bowl. Set aside.

2.    In a large-sized cast-iron wok, heat olive oil over medium-high heat and cook the salmon fillets for about 3-4 minutes per side.

3.    Stir in the honey mixture and immediately remove from heat.

4.    Serve hot.

**Nutrition (Per Serving):** Calories: 305Fat: 17.7g Carbohydrates: 4.7g Fiber: 0.2g Sugar: 4.4g Protein: 33.3g

## 86.Glazed Salmon

❀ ❀ ❀

**Difficulty Level:** Easy
**Servings:** 6
**Preparation Time:** 10 minutes
**Cooking Time:** 18 minutes
**Ingredients:**
- 1 tbsp. Red pepper flakes, crushed
- ⅛ tsp. ground cinnamon
- Ground black pepper, as required
- 6 (6-oz.) fresh salmon fillets
- 2 tbsp. freshly squeezed lemon juice
- 4 tbsp. extra-virgin olive oil, divided
- ¼ c. pure maple syrup
- ¼ c. soy sauce
- ¼ c. scallion, chopped

**Directions:**
1.    In a small-sized bowl, mix all spices and set aside.

2.    In a large-sized bowl, place salmon fillets, lemon juice, two teaspoons of oil, and spice mixture and toss to coat well.

3.    Cover and refrigerate for at least 2 hours.

4.    In a small cast-iron wok, mix maple syrup and soy sauce over medium heat and cook for about 7-10 minutes, stirring occasionally.

5.    Meanwhile, heat the remaining oil over high heat in a large cast-iron wok.

6. Place the salmon fillets, flesh side down, and cook for about 4 minutes.
7. Carefully flip the side and add maple syrup glaze.
8. Cook for about 4 minutes more.
9. Transfer the fillets onto serving plates.
10. Top with the glaze from the pan and serve with the garnishing of the scallion.

**Nutrition (Per Serving):** Calories: 299 Fat: 13.9g Carbohydrates: 10.5g Fiber: 0.5g Sugar: 8.3g Protein: 34.5g

## 87. Sesame Seed Tuna

⅏⅏⅏

**Difficulty Level:** Medium
**Servings:** 2
**Preparation Time:** 10 minutes
**Cooking Time:** 3 minutes
**Ingredients:**
- 2 (4-oz.) ahi tuna steaks
- Salt and ground black pepper, as required
- 4 tbsp. sesame seeds
- 1 tbsp. vegetable oil

**Directions:**
1. Rub the tuna steaks with salt and black pepper evenly.
2. Place the sesame seeds onto a shallow plate.
3. Gently press tuna steaks into seeds to coat evenly.
4. In a medium-sized cast-iron wok, heat oil over medium-high heat and sear the tuna for about 1 minute per side or until desired doneness.
5. Transfer the tuna steaks onto a cutting board.
6. Cut each tuna steak into desired-sized slices and serve.

**Nutrition (Per Serving):** Calories: 372 Fat: 22.9g Carbohydrates: 4.2g Fiber: 2.1g Sugar: 0.1g Protein: 37.1g

## 88. Salmon with Capers

⅏⅏⅏

**Difficulty Level:** Medium
**Servings:** 4
**Preparation Time:** 10 minutes
**Cooking Time:** 8 minutes
**Ingredients:**
- 2 tbsp. olive oil
- 4 (6-oz.) salmon fillets
- 2 tbsp. capers
- Salt and ground black pepper as required
- 4 lemon wedges

**Directions:**
1. In a large-sized cast-iron wok, heat oil over high heat and cook the salmon fillets for about 3 minutes.
2. Sprinkle the salmon fillets with capers, salt, and black pepper.
3. Flip the salmon fillets and cook for about 5 minutes or until browned.
4. Serve with the garnishing of lemon wedges.

**Nutrition (Per Serving):** Calories: 286 Fat: 17.5g Carbohydrates: 0.2g Fiber: 0.1g Sugar: 0g Protein: 33.1g

## 89.Buttered Tilapia

⚜*Occasionally boil some water with baking soda in the cast iron and then rinse and dry quickly to prevent rust*⚜

**Difficulty Level:** Easy
**Servings:** 5
**Preparation Time:** 10 minutes
**Cooking Time:** 8 minutes
**Ingredients:**
- 2 tbsp. unsalted butter
- 5 (5-oz.) tilapia fillets
- 3 garlic cloves, minced
- 1 tbsp. fresh ginger, minced
- 2–3 tbsp. homemade chicken broth
- Salt and ground black pepper, as required

**Directions:**
1. Melt butter in a large-sized cast-iron wok over medium heat and cook the tilapia fillets for about 3 minutes.
2. Flip the side and stir in the garlic and ginger.
3. Cook for about 1-2 minutes.
4. Add the broth and cook for about 2-3 more minutes.
5. Remove from heat and serve hot.

**Nutrition (Per Serving):** Calories: 162 Fat: 5.9g Carbohydrates: 0.8g Fiber: 0.1g Sugar: 0.1g Protein: 26.7g

## 90.Easy Paella

⚜ ⚜ ⚜

**Difficulty Level:** Medium
**Servings:** 2
**Preparation Time:** 5 minutes
**Cooking Time:** 33–35 minutes
**Ingredients:**
- 1 tbsp. olive oil
- 2–3 oz. dried Spanish chorizo, casing removed and chopped
- 2 cloves garlic, minced
- 1 c. Arborio or other short-grain white rice
- 2 c. low-sodium chicken broth
- 1½ c. tomatoes, diced
- Salt and pepper, to taste
- Pinch saffron threads
- ½ c. frozen peas
- ½ lb. shrimp, peeled and deveined

**Directions:**
1. Heat oil in a cast-iron skillet over medium heat. Cook chorizo until browned (about 5 minutes).
2. Add garlic and sauté until fragrant (about 30 seconds). Stir in rice and cook until lightly toasted (about 3 minutes).
3. Stir in broth, tomatoes, salt, pepper, and saffron. Bring to a simmer. Cover and let cook until almost all liquid is absorbed (about 20 minutes).
4. Sprinkle peas over the rice and arrange shrimp on top. Cover and let cook until shrimp are opaque (about 3 minutes).
5. Season with salt and pepper, as needed. Serve immediately.

**Nutrition (Per Serving):** Calories: 560 Fat: 17 g Carbohydrates: 71.2 g Protein: 29.7 g Sodium: 1051 mg

## 91.Almond Crusted Tilapia

⚜ ⚜ ⚜

**Difficulty Level:** Hard
**Servings:** 4
**Preparation Time:** 10 minutes
**Cooking Time:** 10 minutes
**Ingredients:**
- 1 c. almonds, chopped finely and divided

- ¼ c. ground flaxseeds
- 4 (6-oz.) tilapia fillets
- Salt, as required
- 2 tbsp. olive oil

**Directions:**
1. In a shallow bowl, mix ½ c. of almonds and ground flaxseeds.
2. Season the tilapia fillets with the salt evenly.
3. Now, coat the fillets with the almond mixture evenly.
4. Heat the oil over medium heat in a large-sized cast-iron wok and cook the tilapia fillets for about 4 minutes per side.
5. Transfer the tilapia fillets onto a serving plate.
6. In the same wok, add the remaining almonds and cook for about 1 minute, stirring frequently.
7. Remove the almonds from the heat and sprinkle over tilapia.
8. Serve hot.

**Nutrition (Per Serving):** Calories: 374 Fat: 22.6g Carbohydrates: 7.1g Fiber: 4.9g Sugar: 1.1g Protein: 38g

## 92. Cod in Butter Sauce

⚜ ⚜ ⚜

**Difficulty Level:** Easy
**Servings:** 2
**Preparation Time:** 10 minutes
**Cooking Time:** 13minutes
**Ingredients:**
- 2 (6-oz.) cod fillets
- 1 tsp. onion powder
- Salt and ground black pepper, as required
- 3 tbsp. butter, divided
- 2 garlic cloves, minced
- 1-2 lemon slices
- 2 tsp. fresh dill weed

**Directions:**
1. Season each cod fillet evenly with onion powder, salt, and black pepper.
2. In a medium-sized cast-iron wok, melt one tablespoon of butter over high heat and cook the cod fillets for about 4-5 minutes per side.
3. Transfer the cod fillets onto a plate.

4. Meanwhile, melt the remaining butter over low heat in a frying pan and sauté the garlic and lemon slices for 40-60 seconds.
5. Stir in the cooked cod fillets and dill and cook, covered for about 1-2 minutes.
6. Remove the cod fillets from heat and transfer them onto the serving plates.
7. Top with the pan sauce and serve immediately.

**Nutrition (Per Serving):** Calories: 301 Fat: 18.9g Carbohydrates: 2.5g Fiber: 0.3g Sugar: 0.5g Protein: 31.1g

## 93. Cod in Spicy Tomato Sauce

⚜ ⚜ ⚜

**Difficulty Level:** Easy
**Servings:** 5
**Preparation Time:** 15 minutes
**Cooking Time:** 35 minutes
**Ingredients:**
- 1 tsp. dried dill weed
- 2 tsp. sumac
- 2 tsp. ground coriander
- 1½ tsp. ground cumin
- 1 tsp. ground turmeric
- 2 tbsp. extra-virgin olive oil
- 1 large sweet onion, chopped
- 8 garlic cloves, chopped
- 2 jalapeño peppers, chopped
- 5 medium tomatoes, chopped
- 3 tbsp. tomato paste
- 2 tbsp, freshly squeezed lime juice
- ½ c. water
- Salt and ground black pepper, as required
- 5 (6-oz.) boneless cod fillets

**Directions:**
1. Add the dill weed and spices to a small-sized bowl and mix well for the spice mixture.
2. Heat the oil over medium-high heat in a large cast-iron wok and sauté the onion for about 2 minutes.
3. Add the garlic and jalapeño and sauté for about 2 minutes. Stir in the tomatoes, tomato paste, lime juice, water, half of the spice mixture, salt, and pepper, and bring to a boil.
4. Reduce the heat to medium-low and cook, covered for about 10 minutes, stirring occasionally.

5.    Meanwhile, evenly season the cod fillets with the remaining spice mixture, salt, and pepper.

6.    Place the fish fillets into the wok and gently press them into the tomato mixture.

7.    Increase the heat to medium-high and cook for about 2 minutes.

8.    Reduce the heat to medium and cook, covered for about 10-15 minutes or until the desired doneness of the fish. Remove from the heat and serve hot.

**Nutrition (Per Serving):** Calories: 248 Fat: 8.1g Carbohydrates: 12.9g Fiber: 3.2g Sugar: 6g Protein: 33.1g

## 94. Shrimp in Orange Sauce

❧❧❧

**Difficulty Level:** Easy
**Servings:** 4
**Preparation Time:** 15 minutes
**Cooking Time:** 12 minutes
**Ingredients:**

- 2 large egg whites
- 3 tbsp. sesame seeds
- ¼ c. cornstarch
- Salt and ground black pepper, as required
- 1 lb. raw shrimp, peeled and deveined
- 2 tbsp. canola oil
- 1 tsp. white sugar
- ¼ c. dry sherry
- ¾ c. freshly squeezed orange juice
- 2 tbsp. low-sodium soy sauce
- 1 scallion, sliced thinly

**Directions:**

1.    Add egg whites, sesame seeds, cornstarch, salt, and black pepper in a bowl and beat until well combined.

2.    Add shrimp and toss to coat well.

3.    Heat the oil over medium heat in a large-sized cast-iron wok and cook the shrimp for about 2 minutes per side.

4.    With a slotted spoon, transfer the shrimp onto a large plate.

5.    In the same wok, add remaining ingredients except for scallion and bring to a boil.

6.    Cook for about 4-6 minutes, stirring occasionally.

7.    Stir in shrimp and cook for about 1-2 minutes.

8.    Serve hot.

**Nutrition (Per Serving):** Calories: 315 Fat: 12.4g Carbohydrates: 17.7g Fiber: 1.1g Sugar: 5.8g Protein: 29.8g

# CHAPTER 5:

# Vegan And Vegetarian Recipes

## 95.Cabbage with Apple

*❧A dish for vegan food lovers. Follow the step-by-step recipe❧*

**Difficulty Level:** Hard
**Servings:** 5
**Preparation Time:** 15 minutes
**Cooking Time:** 15 minutes
**Ingredients:**
- 2 tsp. coconut oil
- 1 large apple, cored and sliced thinly
- 1 onion, sliced thinly
- 1½ lbs. cabbage, chopped finely
- 1 tbsp. fresh thyme, chopped
- 1 Serrano pepper, chopped
- 1 tbsp. apple cider vinegar
- ⅔ c. almonds, chopped

**Directions:**
1. In a cast-iron wok, melt one teaspoon of coconut oil over medium heat and stir fry the apple for about 2-3 minutes.
2. Transfer the apple into a bowl.
3. In the same wok, melt one teaspoon of coconut oil over medium heat and sauté the onion for about 1-2 minutes.
4. Add the cabbage and stir fry for about 5-7 minutes
5. Add the apple, thyme, and vinegar and cook, covered for about 2 minutes.
6. Serve warm with the garnishing of almonds.

**Nutrition (Per Serving):** Calories: 157 Fat: 8.4g Carbohydrates: 19.3g Fiber: 6.8g Sugar: 10.5g Protein: 4.9g

## 96.Parmesan Quinoa & Asparagus

❧❧❧

**Difficulty Level:** Easy
**Servings:** 4
**Preparation Time:** 15 minutes
**Cooking Time:** 18 minutes
**Ingredients:**
- 1 lb. fresh asparagus, trimmed
- 2 tsp. coconut oil
- ½ of onion, chopped
- 2 garlic cloves, minced
- 1 c. cooked red quinoa
- 1 tbsp. ground turmeric
- ½ c. Parmesan cheese, shredded
- 1 tbsp. freshly squeezed lemon juice

**Directions:**
1. In a large-sized cast-iron saucepan of boiling water, cook the asparagus for about 2-3 minutes.
2. Drain well and rinse under cold water.
3. In a large-sized cast-iron wok, melt coconut oil over medium heat and sauté onion and garlic for about 5 minutes.
4. Stir in quinoa, turmeric, and broth and cook for about 5-6 minutes.
5. Stir in Parmesan, lemon juice, and asparagus and cook for about 3-4 minutes.

**Nutrition (Per Serving):** Calories: 255 Fat: 7.9g Carbohydrates: 35g Fiber: 6.1gSugar: 2.9g Protein: 12.7g

## 97.Mushroom with Spinach

❧❧❧

**Difficulty Level:** Hard
**Servings:** 2
**Preparation Time:** 15 minutes
**Cooking Time:** 12 minutes
**Ingredients:**
- 1 tbsp. olive oil
- ½ tbsp. fresh ginger, grated
- 2 c. fresh mushrooms, sliced
- Salt, as required
- ½ bunch fresh spinach, chopped
- 2 scallions, chopped
- 1 tbsp. soy sauce
- Ground black pepper, as required

**Directions:**
1. Heat oil over medium-high heat and sauté ginger for about 1 minute in a cast-iron wok.
2. Add mushrooms and salt and sauté for about 5-6 minutes.

3.      Add spinach and cook for about 2-3 minutes.

4.      Stir in scallion, soy sauce, and black pepper and cook for about 1-2 minutes.

5.      Serve hot.

**Nutrition (Per Serving):** Calories: 109 Fat: 7.7g Carbohydrates: 8.2g Fiber: 3.3g Sugar: 2.1g Protein: 5.6g

## 98. Ratatouille

❀ ❀ ❀

**Difficulty Level:** Easy
**Servings:** 6
**Preparation Time:** 20 minutes
**Cooking Time:** 53 minutes
**Ingredients:**
- 4 tbsp. of olive oil, divided
- 1 red bell pepper, seeded and chopped
- 1 (26-oz.) jar pasta sauce
- 2 small eggplants, sliced into thin coins
- 2 zucchinis, sliced into thin coins
- 2 yellow squash, sliced into thin coins
- 5 Roma tomatoes, sliced into thin coins
- 2 tbsp. fresh parsley, minced
- 2 tsp. fresh thyme, minced
- 2 tbsp. fresh basil, minced
- 1 tsp. garlic, minced
- Salt and ground black pepper, as required

**Directions:**
1.      Preheat your oven to 375°F.
For the Sauce:
2.      Heat the oil over medium heat in a small cast-iron wok and sauté the bell pepper for about 4-5 minutes.
3.      Reduce the heat to low and stir in the pasta sauce.
4.      Cook for about 2-3 minutes.
5.      Transfer the sauce into a 10-inch cast-iron wok.
6.      Arrange the vegetable coins in a spiral pattern over the sauce
7.      Mix the remaining oil, garlic, herbs, salt, and black pepper in a small-sized bowl.
8.      Place the garlic mixture over vegetables evenly.
9.      Cover the wok and bake for about 25-30 minutes with a piece of foil.

10.      Remove the foil and bake for about 15 minutes more.

11.      Serve hot.

**Nutrition (Per Serving):** Calories: 281 Fat: 13.5g Carbohydrates: 38g Fiber: 12.8g Sugar: 22.3g Protein: 6.8g

## 99. Chickpeas Chili

❀ ❀ ❀

**Difficulty Level:** Hard
**Servings:** 4
**Preparation Time:** 15 minutes
**Cooking Time:** 25 minutes
**Ingredients:**
- 2 tsp. olive oil
- 1 c. onion, chopped
- ½ c. carrot, peeled and chopped
- ¾ c. celery, chopped
- 1 tsp. garlic, minced
- 2 tsp. ground cumin
- 1 tsp. ground ginger
- ½ tsp. ground turmeric
- ⅛ tsp. ground cinnamon
- 2 tsp. Paprika
- ⅛ tsp. red chili powder
- Salt and ground black pepper, as required
- 2 (15½-oz.) cans of chickpeas, rinsed and drained
- 1 (14½-oz.) can of diced tomatoes
- 2 tbsp. tomato paste
- 1½ c. water
- 1 tbsp. freshly squeezed lemon juice
- 2 tbsp. fresh cilantro, chopped

**Directions:**
1.      In a large-sized cast-iron saucepan, heat oil over medium heat and sauté onion, carrot, celery, and garlic for about 5 minutes.
2.      Add spices and sauté for about 1 minute.
3.      Add chickpeas, tomatoes, tomato paste, and water and bring to a boil.
4.      Reduce the heat to low and simmer, covered for about 20 minutes.
5.      Stir in lemon juice and cilantro and remove from heat.
6.      Serve hot.

**Nutrition (Per Serving):** Calories: 339 Fat: 5.6g Carbohydrates: 61.8g Fiber: 13.2g Sugar: 6.1g Protein: 13.2g

## 100.  Summer Squash Gratin

❧❧❧

**Difficulty Level:** Easy
**Servings:** 4
**Preparation Time:** 15 minutes
**Cooking Time:** 35 minutes
**Ingredients:**
- 4 tbsp. olive oil, divided
- ¾ c. panko breadcrumbs
- ½ c. Parmesan cheese, grated
- 2 medium shallots, sliced thinly
- 2 garlic cloves, minced
- 2 lbs. summer squash, cut into ¼-inch pieces crosswise
- 1 tbsp. fresh thyme leaves
- 1 tsp. lemon zest, grated finely
- Salt and ground black pepper, as required

**Directions:**
1. Preheat your oven to 400°F. Arrange a rack in the middle of the oven. In a bowl, add two tablespoons of the oil, breadcrumbs, and Parmesan cheese and mix until well combined.
2. In an 8-inch cast-iron wok, heat the remaining oil over medium heat and cook the shallots for about 3-4 minutes, stirring occasionally. Add the garlic and cook for about 1 minute. Remove from the heat and stir in the squash, thyme, lemon zest, salt, and black pepper.
3. Then, spread the squash mixture into an even layer and sprinkle with the breadcrumbs mixture evenly. Bake for about 25-30 minutes or until the top is golden brown.
4. Remove from the oven and set aside for about 5 minutes before serving.
**Nutrition (Per Serving):** Calories: 283 Fat: 18.5g Carbohydrates: 14.4g Fiber: 2.7g Sugar: 8.1g Protein: 7.2g

## 101.  Glazed Veggies & Apple

❧*Excellent recipe even for non-vegan people*❧

**Difficulty Level:** Easy
**Servings:** 4
**Preparation Time:** 15 minutes
**Cooking Time:** 16 minutes
**Ingredients:**
For the Sauce:
- 1 tsp. fresh ginger, minced
- 2 garlic cloves, minced
- 1 tbsp. fresh orange zest, grated
- ½ c. freshly squeezed orange juice
- 2 tbsp. white wine vinegar
- 2 tbsp. soy sauce
- 1 tbsp. fish sauce

For the Veggies & Apple:
- 1 tbsp. olive oil
- 1 c. carrot, peeled and julienned
- 1 head broccoli, cut into floret
- 1 c. celery, chopped
- 1 c. onion, chopped
- 2 apples, cored and sliced

**Directions:**
For the Sauce:
1. In a large-sized bowl, add all the ingredients and mix until well combined. Set aside.
2. Heat the oil over medium-high heat in a large cast-iron wok and stir fry the carrot and broccoli for about 4-5 minutes.
3. Add the celery and onion and stir fry for about 4-5 minutes.
4. Stir in the sauce and cook for about 2-3 minutes.
5. Stir in the apple slices and cook for about 2-3 minutes more.
6. Serve hot.
**Nutrition (Per Serving):** Calories: 169 Fat: 4.1g Carbohydrates: 31.8g Fiber: 6.4g Sugar: 18.3g Protein: 4.2g

## 102.  Veggies Pie

❧❧❧

**Difficulty Level:** Easy
**Servings:** 4
**Preparation Time:** 20 minutes
**Cooking Time:** 47 minutes
**Ingredients:**
- 3 tbsp. olive oil
- 2 medium red onions, chopped finely
- 1 lb. butternut squash, peeled and cut into ¾-inch pieces
- 1½ tsp. fresh thyme, chopped
- ½ tsp. red pepper flakes, crushed
- 1 bunch Tuscan kale, tough ends removed and sliced thinly
- 3 oz. Parmesan cheese, grated
- 2 large eggs, beaten

- 1 tsp. lemon zest, grated
- Salt and ground black pepper, as required
- 8 oz. frozen phyllo pastry, thawed
- 4 oz. fresh goat cheese, crumbled

**Directions:**
1. Preheat your oven to 400°F. Arrange a rack in the lower third of the oven. Heat the oil over medium heat in a large cast-iron wok and cook the onions for about 6-8 minutes, stirring occasionally.
2. Add the squash and cook for about 8-10 minutes, stirring occasionally. Stir in the thyme and red pepper flakes and transfer the mixture into a medium-sized bowl. Set aside to cool. In the bowl of squash mixture, add the kale, Parmesan, eggs, lemon zest, salt, and black pepper and gently stir to combine. With paper towels, wipe out the same wok.
3. Place the phyllo sheets inside the wok.
4. Place the squash mixture into phyllo and top with the goat cheese in the shape of dots. Brush the edges of phyllo with oil lightly and fold over, filling, overlapping slightly, leaving the center exposed. Place the wok over medium heat and cook for about 3 minutes. Immediately transfer the wok into the oven and bake pie until kale is wilted for about 20-25 minutes. Remove from the oven and set the wok aside for about15 minutes before serving.

**Nutrition (Per Serving):**
Calories: 649 Fat: 30.1g Carbohydrates: 69.3gFiber: 8.1g Sugar: 8g Protein: 29.2g

## 103.     **Herbed Bulgur Pilaf**

❀ ❀ ❀

**Difficulty Level:** Medium
**Servings:** 6
**Preparation Time:** 15 minutes
**Cooking Time:** 40 minutes
**Ingredients:**
- 2 tbsp. extra-virgin olive oil
- 2 c. onion, chopped
- 1 garlic clove, minced
- 1½ c. medium bulgur
- ½ tsp. ground cumin
- ½ tsp. ground turmeric
- 1½ c. carrot, peeled and chopped

- 2 tsp. fresh ginger, grated finely
- Salt, as required
- 2 c. vegetable broth
- 3 tbsp. freshly squeezed lemon juice
- ¼ c. fresh parsley, chopped
- ¼ c. fresh mint leaves, chopped
- ¼ c. fresh dill, chopped
- ½ c. walnuts, toasted and chopped

**Directions:**
1. In a large deep cast-iron wok, heat oil over medium-low heat and cook onion for about 12-15 minutes, stirring occasionally.
2. Add garlic and sauté for about 1 minute.
3. Add bulgur, cumin, and turmeric and stir fry for about 1 minute.
4. Add carrot, ginger, salt, and broth and bring to a boil, stirring occasionally.
5. Simmer, covered for about 15 minute
6. Remove from heat and set aside, covered for about 5 minutes
7. Stir in lemon juice and fresh herbs and serve with the garnishing of walnuts.

**Nutrition (Per Serving):** Calories: 277 Fat: 12.1g Carbohydrates: 36.7g Fiber: 9.4g Sugar: 3.7g Protein: 9.9g

## 104.     **Creamy Zucchini Noodles**

❀ ❀ ❀

**Difficulty Level:** Medium
**Servings:** 4
**Preparation Time:** 15 minutes
**Cooking Time:** 10 minutes
**Ingredients:**
- 1¼ c. heavy whipping cream
- ¼ c. mayonnaise
- Salt and ground black pepper, as required
- 30 oz. zucchini, spiralized with blade C

Lolly Selly Berry

- 4 egg yolks
- 3 oz. Parmesan cheese, grated
- 2 tbsp. fresh parsley, chopped
- 2 tbsp. butter, melted

**Directions:**
1. In a cast-iron saucepan, add the heavy cream and boil.
2. Reduce the heat to low and cook until reduced.
3. Add the mayonnaise, salt, and black pepper and cook until the mixture is warm enough.
4. Add the zucchini noodles and gently stir to combine.
5. Immediately remove from the heat.
6. Place the zucchini noodles mixture onto four serving plates evenly and immediately top with the egg yolks, followed by the parmesan and parsley.
7. Drizzle with butter and serve.
**Nutrition (Per Serving):** Calories: 427 Fat: 39.1g Carbohydrates: 9.7g Fiber: 2.4g Sugar: 3.8g Protein: 13g

## 105. Zucchini Noodles with Mushroom Sauce

**Difficulty Level:** Easy
**Servings:** 5
**Preparation Time:** 20 minutes
**Cooking Time:** 15 minutes
**Ingredients:**
For the Mushroom Sauce:
- 1½ tbsp. butter
- 1 large garlic clove, minced
- 1¼ c. fresh button mushrooms, sliced
- ¼ c. homemade vegetable broth
- ¼ c. heavy cream
- Salt and ground black pepper, as required

For the Zucchini Noodles:
- 3 large zucchinis, spiralized with blade C
- ¼ c. fresh parsley leaves, chopped

**Directions:**
For the Mushroom Sauce:
1. In a large-sized cast-iron wok, melt the butter over medium heat and sauté the garlic for about 1 minute.

2. Stir in the mushrooms and cook for about 6-8 minutes.
3. Stir in the broth and cook for about 2 minutes, stirring continuously.
4. Stir in the cream, salt, and black pepper and cook for about 1 minute.
5. Meanwhile, for the zucchini noodles: in a large-sized cast-iron saucepan of the boiling water, add the zucchini noodles and cook for about 2-3 minutes.
6. Transfer the zucchini noodles into a colander with a slotted spoon and immediately rinse under cold running water.
7. Drain the zucchini noodles well and transfer them onto a large paper towel-lined plate to drain.
8. Divide the zucchini noodles onto serving plates evenly. Remove the mushroom sauce from the heat and evenly place it over zucchini noodles.
9. Serve immediately with the garnishing of parsley.
**Nutrition (Per Serving):** Calories: 77 Fat: 4.6g Carbohydrates: 7.9g Fiber: 2.4g Sugar: 4g Protein: 3.4g

## 106. Broccoli with Cauliflower

**Difficulty Level:** Medium
**Servings:** 6
**Preparation Time:** 15 minutes
**Cooking Time:** 8 minutes
**Ingredients:**
- ½ c. vegetable broth
- 4 c. fresh broccoli florets
- 2 c. fresh cauliflower florets
- 3 shallots, chopped
- 1 tsp. dried basil, crushed
- ½ tsp. seasoned salt
- Ground black pepper, as required

**Directions:**
1. In a large cast-iron wok, add all the ingredients and mix well.
2. Place the wok over medium heat and cook for about 6-8 minutes, stirring occasionally.
3. Serve hot.
**Nutrition (Per Serving):** Calories: 38 Fat: 0.4g Carbohydrates: 7.3g Fiber: 2.4g Sugar: 1.9g Protein: 3g

## 107.  BBQ Baked Beans

*❧Cast iron is a material suitable for any type of cooking. Find out how good vegetables are cooked like in this recipe❧*

**Difficulty Level:** Easy
**Servings:** 4
**Preparation Time:** 15 minutes
**Cooking Time:** 50 minutes
**Ingredients:**
- 1 tbsp. olive oil
- ½ c. green bell pepper, seeded and chopped
- ½ c. white onion, chopped
- 3 garlic cloves, minced
- Salt, as required
- 1¼ c. tomato sauce
- 5 tbsp. pure maple syrup
- ¼ c. water
- 1 tbsp. liquid smoke
- ¼ c. Worcestershire sauce
- Ground black pepper, as required
- 2 (14-oz.) cans of great northern beans, rinsed and drained

**Directions:**
1. Preheat your oven to 325°F.
2. In a large cast-iron wok, heat the oil over medium heat and cook the bell pepper, onion, garlic, and a little salt for about 4-5 minutes.
3. Add the remaining ingredients except for the beans and stir to combine.
4. Add the beans and gently stir to combine.
5. Transfer the wok into the oven and bake for about 30-45 minutes.
6. Serve hot.

**Nutrition (Per Serving):** Calories: 394 Fat: 3.9g Carbohydrates: 75.6g Fiber: 16.2g Sugar: 22g Protein: 16.3g

## 108.  Beans & Quinoa with Veggies

**Difficulty Level:** Medium
**Servings:** 6
**Preparation Time:** 15 minutes
**Cooking Time:** 30 minutes
**Ingredients:**
- 2 c. water
- 1 c. dry quinoa
- 2 tbsp. coconut oil
- 1 medium onion, chopped
- 4 garlic cloves, chopped finely
- 2 tbsp. curry powder
- ½ tsp. ground turmeric
- Cayenne pepper, as required
- Salt, as required
- 2 c. broccoli, chopped
- 1 c. fresh kale, trimmed and chopped
- 1 c. green peas, shelled
- 1 red bell pepper, seeded and chopped
- 2 c. canned kidney beans, rinsed and drained
- 2 tbsp. freshly squeezed lime juice

**Directions:**
1. In a pan, add the water and boil over high heat.
2. Add the quinoa and stir to combine.
3. Reduce the heat to low and simmer for about 10-15 minutes or until all the liquid is absorbed.
4. In a large cast-iron wok, melt the coconut oil over medium heat and sauté the onion, garlic, curry powder, turmeric, and salt for about 4-5 minutes.
5. Add the vegetables and cook for about 4-5 minutes.
6. Stir in the quinoa and beans and cook for about 2-3 minutes.
7. Drizzle with the lime juice and serve hot.

**Nutrition (Per Serving):** Calories: 270 Fat: 6.8g Carbohydrates: 42.1g Fiber: 12.3g Sugar: 3.8g Protein: 12.6g

## 109. Carrots with Snow Peas

❧❧❧

**Difficulty Level:** Hard
**Servings:** 4
**Preparation Time:** 15 minutes
**Cooking Time:** 6 minutes
**Ingredients:**
- 2 tbsp. butter
- 1¾ c. fresh carrots, peeled and sliced
- 2¾ c. fresh snow peas
- 1 shallot, minced
- Salt, as required
- 1 tbsp. vegetable broth

**Directions:**
1. In a large cast-iron wok, melt the butter over medium heat and stir fry the carrots for about 3 minutes. Add the snow peas, shallot, and salt and stir fry for about 2 minutes.
2. Stir in the broth and stir fry for about 1 minute. Remove from the heat and serve hot.
**Nutrition (Per Serving):** Calories: 121 Fat: 6g Carbohydrates: 13.3g Fiber: 4.3g Sugar: 6.8g Protein: 4.2g

## 110. Couscous with Cauliflower & Dates

❧❧❧

**Difficulty Level:** Easy
**Servings:** 4
**Preparation Time:** 10 minutes
**Cooking Time:** 10 minutes
**Ingredients:**
- 2 tbsp. olive oil, divided
- 2 garlic cloves, minced

- 1¼ c. vegetable broth
- 1 c. pearl couscous
- 1 tbsp. freshly squeezed lemon juice
- 1 shallot, chopped
- 2 c. cauliflower florets
- Salt and ground black pepper, as required
- 3 tbsp. dates, pitted and chopped
- 1 tsp. red wine vinegar
- 2 tbsp. fresh parsley, chopped

**Directions:**
1. Heat the oil over medium-high heat in a large cast-iron wok and sauté the onion for about 4-5 minutes. Add the parsnip and carrot and sauté for about 4-5 minutes.
2. Add the zucchini, yellow squash, garlic, and spices and sauté for about 4-5 minutes.
3. Stir in the couscous and cook for about 2 minutes, stirring occasionally.
4. Stir in the apricots and broth and cook, covered for about 5 minutes or until all the liquid is absorbed. Remove from the heat, and with a fork, fluff the couscous completely.
5. Stir in the cilantro and almonds and serve.
**Nutrition (Per Serving):** Calories: 494 Fat: 18g Carbohydrates: 69g Fiber: 8.8g Sugar: 7.7g Protein: 16g

## 111. Spicy & Nutty Quinoa

❧❧❧

**Difficulty Level:** Easy
**Servings:** 4
**Preparation Time:** 10 minutes
**Cooking Time:** 25 minutes
**Ingredients:**
- 2 tbsp. olive oil
- 1 tsp. curry powder
- 1 tsp. ground turmeric
- ½ tsp. ground cumin
- 1 c. uncooked quinoa, rinsed and drained
- 2 c. vegetable broth
- ¾ c. almonds, toasted
- ½ c. raisins
- ¾ c. fresh parsley, chopped

**Directions:**
1. In a medium-sized cast-iron saucepan, heat oil over medium-low heat and sauté the curry powder, turmeric, and cumin for about 1-2 minutes.

2. Add the quinoa and sauté for about 2-3 minutes.

3. Add the broth and stir to combine.

4. Adjust the heat to low and simmer, covered for about 20 minutes.

5. Remove the saucepan from heat and set aside, covered for about 5 minutes.

6. In the pan of quinoa mixture, add almonds and raisins and toss to coat.

7. Drizzle with lemon juice and serve.

**Nutrition (Per Serving):** Calories: 402 Fat: 19.5g Carbohydrates: 47.4g Fiber: 6.6g Sugar: 12g Protein: 13.2g

## 112.    **Pasta with Tomatoes**

❖❖❖

**Difficulty Level:** Easy
**Servings:** 4
**Preparation Time:** 15 minutes
**Cooking Time:** 15 minutes
**Ingredients:**
- 8 oz. pasta
- 2 tbsp. olive oil
- 1 tbsp. garlic, minced
- 1 tbsp. dried oregano, crushed
- 1 tbsp. dried basil, crushed
- 1 tsp. dried thyme, crushed
- 2 c. cherry tomatoes, halved

**Directions:**
1. In a large-sized saucepan of lightly salted boiling water, add the pasta and cook for about 8-10 minutes or according to the package's directions.

2. Drain the pasta well.

3. Heat oil over medium heat in a large cast-iron wok and sauté the garlic for about 1 minute.

4. Stir in the herbs and sauté for about 1 minute more.

5. Add the pasta and cook for about 2-3 minutes or heated completely.

6. Fold in tomatoes and remove from heat.

7. Serve hot.

**Nutrition (Per Serving):** Calories: 247 Fat: 8.6g Carbohydrates: 36.1g Fiber: 1.7g Sugar: 2.4g Protein: 7.5g

## 113.    **Veggies Paella**

❖*Paella is a vegetarian dish that cooks very well in cast iron and maintains its excellent flavors*❖

**Difficulty Level:** Easy **Servings:** 4 **Preparation Time:** 20 minutes **Cooking Time:** 20 minutes
**Ingredients:**
- 1 c. short-grain brown rice
- Pinch of saffron
- 3 tbsp. warm water
- 6 c. low-sodium vegetable broth
- 1 tbsp. olive oil
- 1 large yellow onion, chopped
- 1 medium red bell pepper, seeded and sliced
- 1 medium yellow bell pepper, seeded and sliced
- 4 garlic cloves, sliced thinly
- ¾ c. fresh tomatoes, crushed
- 2 tbsp. tomato paste
- ½ tbsp. hot paprika
- 1 c. green beans, trimmed and halved
- 3 artichoke hearts, sliced
- 1 c. cooked chickpeas
- ¼ c. frozen green peas
- ¼ c. fresh parsley, chopped
- Salt and ground black pepper, as required

**Directions:**
1. In a large-sized cast-iron saucepan of the salted boiling water, add the rice and cook for about 20 minutes. Drain the rice and set it aside. In a small-sized bowl, mix the saffron threads and warm water. Set aside.

2. In a small pan, add the broth and bring to a gentle simmer. Reduce the heat to low to keep the broth warm. Meanwhile, heat the oil and sauté the onions in a large cast-iron wok for about 4-5 minutes.

3. Add the bell peppers and garlic slices and cook for about 7 minutes. Stir in the saffron mixture, tomatoes, tomato paste, paprika, salt, and black pepper, and cook for about 2-3 minutes. Add the green beans, artichoke, and chickpeas and stir to combine. Stir in the cooked rice and broth and bring to a boil. Simmer for about 20 minutes or until all the liquid is absorbed. Stir in the green peas and parsley and cover the pan. Remove from the heat and set aside, covered for about 5-10 minutes before serving.

**Nutrition (Per Serving):** Calories: 413 Fat: 7.6g Carbohydrates: 71.2g Fiber: 19.9g Sugar: 14g Protein: 20.7g

## 114. Veggies Curry

✤✤✤

**Difficulty Level:** Hard
**Servings:** 4
**Preparation Time:** 15 minutes
**Cooking Time:** 25 minutes
**Ingredients:**
- 2 tsp. coconut oil
- 1 small white onion, chopped
- 2 garlic cloves, chopped finely
- 1 tbsp. fresh ginger, chopped finely
- Salt, as required
- 3 carrots, peeled and cut into ¾-inch round slices
- 2 c. asparagus, trimmed and cut into 2-inch pieces
- 2 tbsp. green curry paste
- 1½ tsp. coconut sugar
- 1 (14-oz.) can of coconut milk
- ½ c. water
- 2 c. fresh baby spinach, chopped roughly
- 1½ tsp. soy sauce
- 1½ tsp. balsamic vinegar
- Red pepper flakes, as required

**Directions:**
1. In a large cast-iron wok, melt the coconut oil over medium heat and sauté the onion, garlic, ginger, and a pinch of salt for about 5 minutes.
2. Add the carrots and asparagus and cook for about 3 minutes, stirring occasionally.
3. Stir in the curry paste and cook for about 2 minutes, stirring occasionally.

4. Add the coconut sugar, milk, and water, and bring a gentle simmer.
5. Cook for about 5-10 minutes or until the desired doneness of vegetables.
6. Stir in the spinach and cook for about 1 minute.
7. Stir in soy sauce, vinegar, salt, and red pepper flakes and remove from heat.
8. Serve hot.

**Nutrition (Per Serving):** Calories: 327 Fat: 27.7g Carbohydrates: 20.9g Fiber: 5.6g Sugar: 9.2g Protein: 5.1g

## 115. Rice Noodles with Snow Peas

✤✤✤

**Difficulty Level:** Hard
**Servings:** 2
**Preparation Time:** 15 minutes
**Cooking Time:** 10 minutes
**Ingredients:**
For the Spicy Sauce:
- 2 garlic cloves, minced
- 1 tbsp. coconut sugar
- ½ tsp. red pepper flakes, crushed
- 2 tbsp. freshly squeezed lime juice
- 2 tbsp. soy sauce

For the Noodles:
- 6 oz. thin rice noodles
- 2 tbsp. sesame oil, toasted and divided
- 1 small red bell pepper, seeded and sliced thinly
- ¼ of yellow onion, sliced thinly 12 snow peas
- 4 tsp. curry powder, divided
- 1 tbsp. soy sauce

For the Topping:
1. 2 scallions, sliced thinly

**Directions:**
For the Sauce:
2. In a bowl, add all the ingredients and beat until well combined. Set aside.
3. In a large-sized bowl of very hot water, add the noodles and set them aside, cover for about 5-10 minutes or prepare according to the package's directions.
4. Drain the noodles and then cut them into 3-inch pieces. Set aside.

5.	Heat one tablespoon of peanut oil in a large cast-iron wok over medium-high heat and sauté the bell pepper and onion for about 4 minutes.
6.	Add the snow peas, two teaspoons of curry powder, and soy sauce and sauté for about 2-3 minutes.
7.	Transfer the vegetable mixture into a large-sized bowl.
8.	Heat the remaining oil over medium heat in the same wok and cook the noodles, sauce, and remaining curry powder for about 1 minute.
9.	Return the vegetable mixture to the wok with noodles and cook for about 1-2 minutes, tossing occasionally.
10.	Divide the noodle mixture onto serving plates and top with scallion.
11.	Serve immediately.

**Nutrition (Per Serving):** Calories: 306 Fat: 14.7g Carbohydrates: 41g Fiber: 4.6g   Sugar: 11.3g Protein: 4.7g

# CHAPTER 6:

# Sweet Cakes And Frutta Caramellata Recipes

## 116. Banana-Pecan Clafoutis

*If you like fruit but especially bananas, try this recipe at least once*

**Difficulty Level:** Easy
**Servings:** 8 servings
**Preparation Time:** 15 minutes
**Cooking Time:** 45 minutes
**Ingredients:**
- 1 c. whole milk
- ¼ c. whipping cream
- 3 eggs
- ½ c. granulated sugar
- 1 tsp. vanilla extract
- 2 tbsp. butter, melted
- ¼ tsp. salt
- ½ c. all-purpose flour
- 2 bananas, peeled and thinly sliced
- 2 tsp. fresh lemon juice
- ½ c. pecans, roughly chopped

**Directions:**
1. Preheat the oven to 350°F.
2. Whisk together milk, cream, eggs, sugar, extract, butter, and salt. Add the flour and whisk gently until incorporated.
3. Place sliced bananas in a bowl with lemon juice.
4. Lightly grease a cast-iron skillet and heat in the oven for 5 minutes. Remove skillet and pour in batter. Scatter bananas and pecans over batter and place in oven. Bake until golden and puffed, about 35 minutes.

**Nutrition (Per Serving):** Calories: 194 Sodium: 131 mg Dietary Fiber: 1.1 g Total Fat: 8.2 g Total Carbohydrates: 27.2 g Protein: 4.5 g.

## 117. Apple Dutch Baby Pancake

**Difficulty Level:** Easy
**Servings:** 4-6 servings
**Preparation Time:** 15 minutes
**Cooking Time:** 20 minutes
**Ingredients:**
- 3 large eggs, room temperature
- ¾ c. whole milk
- ¾ c. all-purpose flour
- 1 tsp. almond extract
- ¼ tsp. salt
- 2 large Granny Smith apples, peeled, cored, and sliced
- 1 tbsp. sugar
- 1 tsp. cinnamon
- ½ tsp. ginger
- 4 tbsp. butter, divided
- 2 tbsp. light brown sugar

**Directions:**
1. Preheat oven to 400°F.
2. Whisk together eggs, milk, flour, extract, and salt.
3. Place sliced apples in a bowl with sugar, cinnamon, and ginger.
4. Melt two tablespoons of butter in a heated cast-iron skillet. Sprinkle brown sugar inside the skillet. Add apples and cook until apples have softened. Transfer to a plate.
5. Wipe out the skillet and melt the remaining two tablespoons of butter. Make sure to coat the sides of the skillet as well. When the skillet is very hot, add apples and pour the batter inside the skillet. Bake until puffed and golden, about 13-15 minutes.

**Nutrition (Per Serving):** Calories: 240 Sodium: 201 mg Dietary Fiber: 2.4 g Total Fat: 11.4 g Total Carbohydrates: 29.2 g Protein: 6.0 g.

## 118. Blueberry Slump

**Difficulty Level:** Medium
**Servings:** 8 servings
**Preparation Time:** 15 minutes
**Cooking Time:** 30 minutes
**Ingredients:**
- 2 lbs. fresh blueberries
- ⅓ c. sugar
- 2 tbsp. water
- 1 ½ tbsp. fresh lime juice
- 1 c. all-purpose flour
- 1 tsp. baking powder
- 1 tsp. baking soda
- ¼ tsp. kosher salt
- ½ c. buttermilk
- 2 tbsp. unsalted butter, melted
- 1 tsp. turbinado sugar

**Directions:**
1. If cooking indoors, preheat the oven to 375°F.

2.    Preheat cast-iron skillet over medium heat. Cook blueberries, sugar, water, and lime juice for 10-15 minutes, or until the fruit breaks down and thickens.

3.    In a separate bowl, whisk together flour, baking powder, baking soda, salt, and an additional 1 ½ tablespoons sugar. Add buttermilk and melted butter and stir until a moist dough forms.

4.    Scoop dough evenly over the fruit mixture in skillet. Sprinkle turbinado sugar on top. Bake in an oven or on top of the grill for 20-25 minutes until dough sets.

**Nutrition (Per Serving):** Calories:  188 Sodium: 271 mg Dietary Fiber: 3.2 g Total Fat: 3.5 g Total Carbohydrates: 38.5 g Protein: 3.0 g.

## 119.    Bourbon Pecan Pie

⚜Pecans are a great natural antioxidant. Try this recipe using cast iron⚜

**Difficulty Level:** Easy
**Servings:** 8 servings
**Preparation Time:** 20 minutes
**Cooking Time:** 2 hours and 30 minutes
**Ingredients:**
- ½ package refrigerated pie crust
- 1 tbsp. brown sugar
- 4 large eggs
- 1 ½ c. white sugar
- ½ c. melted butter
- ½ c. chopped toasted pecans
- 2 tbsp. all-purpose flour
- 1 tbsp. cream
- 1 ½ tsp. bourbon
- ½ tsp. vanilla extract
- 2 c. pecan halves

**Directions:**
1.    Preheat oven to 350°F.
2.    Form pie crust to fit a 10-inch greased cast iron skillet. Sprinkle with brown sugar. Pierce crust and bake for 10 minutes until golden brown.
3.    Whisk eggs, white sugar, melted butter, chopped pecans, flour, cream, bourbon, and vanilla extract in a large bowl. Pour into pie crust and top with pecan halves, arranged in concentric circles.
4.    Transfer the skillet to the oven and bake for 25-30 minutes. Turn oven off and let pie stand in oven with the door closed for 2 hours.

**Nutrition (Per Serving):**  Calories:  346 Sodium: 137 mg Dietary Fiber: 0.6 g Total Fat: 18.9 g Total Carbohydrates: 42.6 g Protein: 4.1 g.

## 120.    Rustic Blackberry Galette

⚜ ⚜ ⚜

**Difficulty Level:** Easy
**Servings:** 6 servings
**Preparation Time:** 15 minutes
**Cooking Time:** 45 minutes
**Ingredients:**
- 2 lbs. fresh blackberries, rinsed and dried
- ¾ c. granulated sugar
- 2 tbsp. fresh lime juice
- 2 tsp. chopped fresh basil
- 1 tsp. chopped fresh mint
- Pinch of salt
- ¼ tsp. cinnamon
- 1 tsp. vanilla extract
- 1 package store-bought puff pastry, thawed
- 1 egg white, slightly beaten

**Directions:**
1.    Preheat oven to 375°F. Roll out puff pastry and place in greased cast iron skillet. Allow pastry to hang over the sides slightly.
2.    Toss together blackberries, sugar, lime juice, basil, mint, salt, cinnamon, and vanilla extract.
3.    Spread fruit mixture inside pastry dough in skillet. Fold pastry over the berries to cover edges and about ½ way up. Brush egg white over pastry. Place skillet in oven and bake about 40 minutes, until pastry browns.

**Nutrition (Per Serving):**  Calories:  211 Sodium: 27 mg Dietary Fiber: 8.3 g Total Fat: 3.7 g Total Carbohydrates: 44.5 g Protein: 3.3 g.

## 121. Deep-Dish Giant Double Chocolate Chip Cookie

❧❧❧

**Difficulty Level:** Easy
**Servings:** 6-8 servings
**Preparation Time:** 15 minutes
**Cooking Time:** 30 minutes
**Ingredients:**
- ½ c. unsalted butter
- ½ c. light brown sugar
- ½ c. white sugar
- 1 tsp. vanilla
- 1 large egg
- 1 c. all-purpose flour
- ½ tsp. baking powder
- ½ tsp. salt
- 1 c. chocolate chip
- ½ c. chocolate chunks

**Directions:**
1. Preheat oven to 350°F.
2. Preheat a 10-inch skillet. Melt butter over low heat.
3. Add sugars and stir well. Incorporate vanilla and egg and beat quickly to make sure eggs do not cook. Stir in flour, baking soda, and salt. Fold in chocolate chips and chunks and spread the dough out in a skillet lightly with a spatula to flatten.
4. Bake for 25 minutes until cookie appears browned on top.

**Nutrition (Per Serving):** Calories: 417 Sodium: 299 mg Dietary Fiber: 1.4 g Total Fat: 21.1 g Total carbohydrates: 53.2 g Protein: 4.9 g.

## 122. Apple-Cinnamon Skillet Cake

**Difficulty Level:** Easy
**Servings:** 6-8 servings
**Preparation Time:** 15 minutes
**Cooking Time:** 50 minutes
**Ingredients:**
- 1 c. all-purpose flour
- ½ tsp. baking powder
- ½ tsp. baking soda
- ½ tsp. salt
- 4 tbsp. unsalted butter, room temperature
- ¾ c. granulated sugar
- 2 large eggs
- ½ c. milk
- 2 apples, any variety, peeled, cored, and sliced
- Cinnamon- sugar mixture (5 tbsp. sugar, mixed with 1 ½ tsp. cinnamon)

**Directions:**
1. Preheat oven to 350°F.
2. Grease a cast-iron skillet with butter or cooking spray.
3. Whisk together flour, baking powder, baking soda, and salt. Beat butter and sugar at medium speed with a hand mixer in a separate bowl. Beat in eggs. Add flour mixture and milk in several additions, alternating with each addition.
4. Pour batter into the skillet. Bake for 15 minutes and remove from oven. Fan apples over the batter with cinnamon sugar mixture on top. Bake until the top is set and golden brown, another 30 minutes.

**Nutrition (Per Serving):** Calories: 228 Sodium: 293 mg Dietary Fiber: 1.5 g Total Fat: 7.5 g Total Carbohydrates: 38.0 g Protein: 3.9 g

## 123. Sweet Cherry Clafouti

❧*Take care of your cast iron skillet. It is an eternal material if it is properly maintained*❧
**Difficulty Level:** Medium
**Servings:** 8 servings
**Preparation Time:** 15 minutes
**Cooking Time:** 45 minutes
**Ingredients:**
- 1 c. whole milk

- ¼ c. whipping cream
- 3 eggs
- ½ c. granulated sugar
- 1 tsp. almond extract
- 2 tbsp. butter, melted
- ½ c. all-purpose flour
- 2 c. cherries, pitted and sliced
- Powdered sugar

**Directions:**
1.　Preheat the oven to 350°F.
2.　Whisk together milk, cream, eggs, sugar, extract, and butter. Add the flour and whisk gently until incorporated.
3.　Lightly grease a cast-iron skillet and heat in the oven for 5 minutes. Remove skillet and pour in batter. Scatter cherries all around batter and place in oven. Bake until golden and puffed, about 35 minutes. Dust with powdered sugar.
**Nutrition (Per Serving):** Calories: 326 Sodium: 84 mg Dietary Fiber: 1.1 g Total Fat: 6.8 g Total Carbohydrates: 61.8 g Protein: 4.5 g

## 124.　Gooey Chocolate Fudge Cake

✦✦✦

**Difficulty Level:** Hard
**Servings:** 8 servings
**Preparation Time:** 15 minutes
**Cooking Time:** 25 minutes
**Ingredients:**
- 1 c. flour
- ½ tsp. baking soda
- 1 c. sugar
- Pinch of salt
- ½ c. vegetable oil
- 3 tbsp. cocoa powder

- ½ c. water
- ¼ c. whole milk
- 1 egg
- 1 tsp. vanilla extract

**Directions:**
1.　Preheat the oven to 350°F.
2.　Whisk together flour, baking soda, sugar, and salt in a large bowl.
3.　Combine oil, cocoa powder, and water in another bowl. Whisk in flour mixture and pour into skillet.
4.　Incorporate milk, egg, and vanilla into the batter.
5.　Add to skillet and bake for 25 minutes, or until the edges are set and the center is slightly jiggly.
**Nutrition (Per Serving):** Calories: 290 Sodium: 91 mg Dietary Fiber: 1.0 g Total Fat: 14.9 g Total Carbohydrates: 38.5 g Protein: 2.9 g

## 125.　Grilled Fruit Medley

**Difficulty Level:** Medium
**Servings:** 4-6 servings
**Preparation Time:** 5 minutes
**Cooking Time:** 5 minutes
**Ingredients:**
- Cooking spray
- 2 tbsp. avocado oil
- 1 ½ tbsp. sugar
- ¼ tsp. sea salt
- 2 large peaches or nectarines, cut into wedges
- 5 thick slices of watermelon, with rinds removed
- 3 thick slices of pineapple, cut into sticks
- 2 tsp. fresh lime juice
- 2 tbsp. chopped mint
- 1 c. blueberries

**Directions:**
1.　Heat a cast-iron skillet over medium-high heat. Spray with cooking spray. Dab a small amount of oil onto the fruit. Sprinkle on sugar and sea salt.
2.　Place peach wedges, watermelon, and pineapple into skillet, working in batches. Cook for 1-2 minutes on each side until slightly charred and softened.

3.      Place fruit on a platter and sprinkle with lime juice, chopped mint, and blueberries.

**Nutrition (Per Serving):** Calories: 169 Sodium: 83 mg Dietary Fiber: 3.8 g Total Fat: 1.2 g Total Carbohydrates: 41.9 g Protein: 2.7 g.

## 126.      Three Berry Crumble

⚜⚜⚜

**Difficulty Level:** Easy
**Servings:** 8 servings
**Preparation Time:** 15 minutes
**Cooking Time:** 1 hour
**Ingredients:**
- 6 c. of fresh mixed berries, washed and dried
- ¼ c. of sugar
- ¼ c. of flour
- 1 tbsp. lemon juice
- ¾ c. flour
- ¾ c. brown sugar
- ¾ c. old fashioned oats
- ½ c. chopped almonds
- 1 tsp. cinnamon
- 1 stick cold butter, cut into cubes

**Directions:**
1.      Preheat oven to 375°F.
2.      Lightly toss the berries, sugar, flour, and lemon juice inside your cast iron skillet.
3.      Mix the flour, brown sugar, oats, almonds, and cinnamon in a bowl. Incorporate cold butter with your fingertips into the oat mixture until small clumps form.
4.      Pour topping onto fruit and bake for 45 minutes to 1 hour, until bubbles form and top appears browned and crispy. Serve with vanilla ice cream right out of the skillet.

**Nutrition (Per Serving):** Calories: 387 Sodium: 86 mg Dietary Fiber: 6.5 g Total Fat: 15.9 g Total Carbohydrates: 55.9 g Protein: 5.7 g.

## 127.      Hazelnut Cream  Brownies

⚜⚜⚜

**Difficulty Level:** Easy
**Servings:** 8 servings
**Preparation Time:** 15 minutes
**Cooking Time:** 50 minutes
**Ingredients:**
- 1 c. sugar
- 3 large eggs
- 1 c. all-purpose flour
- ½ c. Dutch cocoa powder
- ½ tsp. salt
- ½ tsp. vanilla extract
- ½ stick unsalted butter
- ¼ c. half and half
- 4 oz. chocolate chips
- ½ c. Hazelnut Cream  spread

**Directions:**
1.      Preheat oven to 350°F.
2.      Whisk together sugar and eggs in one bowl. Whisk together flour, cocoa, and salt in another bowl.
3.      In a cast-iron skillet, simmer butter and half and a half together over low heat. Add chocolate chips and stir until melted, about 2 minutes. Add in Hazelnut Cream  and continue stirring until incorporated. Remove from heat.
4.      Pour sugar mixture into chocolate mixture in skillet. Carefully add flour mixture and fold until just incorporated.
5.      Bake for 25 minutes but start checking at 20 minutes. At about 20-22 minutes, you will have a brownie with a fudge-like consistency.

**Nutrition (Per Serving):** Calories: 429 Sodium: 271 mg Dietary Fiber: 2.4 g Total Fat: 19.8 g Total Carbohydrates: 58.4 g Protein: 6.3 g.

## 128.    Oatmeal Cherry and Pecan Skillet Cookie

❦*This recipe is suitable for 8 servings but beware even one person could eat it all. A really delicious recipe*❦

**Difficulty Level:** Easy
**Servings:** 8 servings
**Preparation Time:** 15 minutes
**Cooking Time:** 25 minutes
**Ingredients:**
- ½ c. unsalted butter
- 1 c. brown sugar
- 1 egg
- ½ tsp. baking soda
- Pinch of salt
- 1 tsp. cinnamon
- ¼ tsp. nutmeg
- 1 ¼ c. all-purpose flour
- ½ c. quick-cooking oatmeal
- ½ c. toasted pecans, chopped
- 1 c. dried cherries, chopped in half

**Directions:**
1. Preheat oven to 375°F.
2. Heat a cast-iron skillet over medium heat. Melt the butter for several minutes until it foams. Stir in brown sugar. Remove from heat for several minutes. Add egg, baking soda, salt, cinnamon, and nutmeg to the skillet and whisk with sugar. Add flour and stir until just incorporated.
3. Add oatmeal, pecans, and cherries and combine well. Pat cookie dough in the skillet to flatten. Bake for 15-18 minutes or until set.
**Nutrition (Per Serving):** Calories: 293 Sodium: 176 mg Dietary Fiber: 1.4 g Total Fat: 14.0 g Total Carbohydrates: 39.2 g Protein: 3.7 g

## 129.    Peach Cobbler

❦ ❦ ❦

**Difficulty Level:** Easy
**Servings:** 8 servings
**Preparation Time:** 15 minutes
**Cooking Time:** 1 hour

**Ingredients:**
- 1 ½ c. all-purpose flour
- 1 tsp. sugar
- ¼ tsp. fine sea salt
- 1 stick cold butter, cut into pieces
- 5 to 6 tbsp. cold water
- ¼ c. all-purpose flour
- 1 c. light brown sugar
- ½ lemon, juiced
- 4 ½ c. peaches, sliced into thin wedges
- 3 tbsp. sugar
- 1 tbsp. cinnamon

**Directions:**
1. Preheat oven to 375°F.
2. To make the crust, mix flour, sugar, and salt. Cut in butter with your fingertips. Add water, one tablespoon at a time, until the mixture is moist. Only pour enough water to make sure dough sticks together.
3. Place dough on a floured surface and roll out dough to one-quarter inch thickness. Place dough in an oiled 10-inch cast-iron skillet. Pierce dough with a fork. Bake for about 8-10 minutes or until browned. Remove from oven.
4. Combine flour, brown sugar, lemon juice, and peaches in a separate bowl. Toss to coat thoroughly. Pour into prepared crust. Sprinkle with cinnamon-sugar mixture. Bake 40 minutes or until crust is golden and peaches are bubbly.
**Nutrition (Per Serving):** Calories: 328 Sodium: 146 mg Dietary Fiber: 2.6 g Total Fat: 12.0 g Total Carbohydrates: 53.5 g Protein: 3.9 g

Lolly Selly Berry

## 130. Strawberry Rhubarb Upside-Down Cake

⚜ ⚜ ⚜

**Difficulty Level:** Easy
**Servings:** 8 servings
**Preparation Time:** 15 minutes
**Cooking Time:** 30 minutes
**Ingredients:**
- 1 c. light brown sugar, divided
- ⅓ c. unsalted butter, melted
- 2 c. red rhubarb, chopped into cubes
- 1 pt. fresh strawberries washed and hulled, cut in half
- 1 c. whole wheat flour
- ½ tsp. baking powder
- Pinch of salt
- 3 eggs
- ½ c. white sugar
- ½ tsp. vanilla extract
- ¼ tsp. cinnamon
- Chopped mint leaves and whipped cream for garnish

**Directions:**
1. Preheat the oven to 350°F.
2. Combine ½ c. brown sugar and melted butter and pour in skillet, coating bottom of skillet thoroughly.
3. Arrange strawberries and rhubarb in the skillet, filling all the spaces.
4. Mix flour, baking powder, and salt in a bowl. In another bowl, beat eggs and gradually add white sugar and ½ c. brown sugar. Continue beating until light and fluffy. Add vanilla extract and cinnamon and beat one more minute.
5. At low speed, add flour mixture to egg mixture and beat until combined. Spread the batter over the fruit carefully to not move the fruit. Make sure the batter covers the fruit entirely.
6. Bake until the top of the cake is set and golden. Remove the skillet from the oven and run a knife around the edges. Invert onto a platter and wait a couple of minutes before pulling away from the skillet. Top with fresh mint and whipped cream.

**Nutrition (Per Serving):** Calories: 286 Sodium: 85 mg Dietary Fiber: 1.9 g Total Fat: 9.7 g Total Carbohydrates: 47.4 g Protein: 4.4 g

## 131. Sweet Cornbread Wedges

⚜ ⚜ ⚜

**Difficulty Level:** Hard
**Servings:** 8 servings
**Preparation Time:** 15 minutes
**Cooking Time:** 20 minutes
**Ingredients:**
- 1 stick of unsalted butter
- 1 ½ c. ground yellow cornmeal
- ½ c. all-purpose flour
- 1 tsp. baking powder
- ½ tsp. baking soda
- 3 tbsp. granulated sugar
- ½ tsp. salt
- 2 large eggs
- 1 ½ c. buttermilk
- ½ c. frozen corn, thawed

**Directions:**
1. Preheat oven to 400°F.
2. Melt five tablespoons of butter in the microwave.
3. Whisk together cornmeal, flour, baking powder, baking soda, sugar, and salt.
4. In a separate bowl, beat eggs until light and pale yellow. Whisk in buttermilk. Pour wet mixture into dry mixture and lightly incorporate until no dry streaks remain. Fold in melted butter until just combined. Add corn kernels.
5. Preheat cast-iron skillet over low to medium heat. Place the remaining three tablespoons of butter in a skillet and melt. Pour batter into the hot skillet and bake in the oven until golden brown, about 15 minutes. Cut into wedges.

**Nutrition (Per Serving):** Calories: 204 Sodium: 375 mg Dietary Fiber: 0.8 g Total Fat: 13.4 g Total Carbohydrates: 17.7 g Protein: 4.7 g.

## 132. Traditional Apple Pie

⚜ ⚜ ⚜

**Difficulty Level:** Easy
**Servings:** 6-8 servings
**Preparation Time:** 15 minutes
**Cooking Time:** 1 hour and 5 minutes
**Ingredients:**
- 4 lbs. apples (such as Braeburn, Granny Smith, or Golden delicious), peeled, cored, and sliced into ½ inch thick wedges
- 1 tsp. ground cinnamon

- ¼ tsp. apple pie spice
- ¾ c. granulated sugar
- 3 tsp. lemon juice
- 6 tbsp. butter
- ¾ c. brown sugar
- 1 package of refrigerated pie crusts
- 1 egg white
- 1 ½ tbsp. turbinado sugar

**Directions:**

1.    Preheat oven to 350°F.

2.    Toss peeled apples with cinnamon, apple pie spice, sugar, and lemon juice in a bowl.

3.    Melt butter in a cast-iron skillet over low to medium heat and add brown sugar. Cook for 2 minutes until sugar dissolves. Remove heat and spread one pie crust in a skillet over melted sugar.

4.    Pour in the apple mixture and spread evenly. Top with remaining piecrust. Whisk egg white and brush piecrust with egg white. Sprinkle top with turbinado sugar. Cut in several slits on top crust.

5.    Bake for 45 minutes to 1 hour or until the fruit mixture bubbles. Cover with foil if edges begin to darken.

**Nutrition (Per Serving):** Calories: 340 Sodium: 90 mg Dietary Fiber: 5.7 g Total Fat: 9.9 g Total Carbohydrates: 67.0 g Protein: 1.3 g

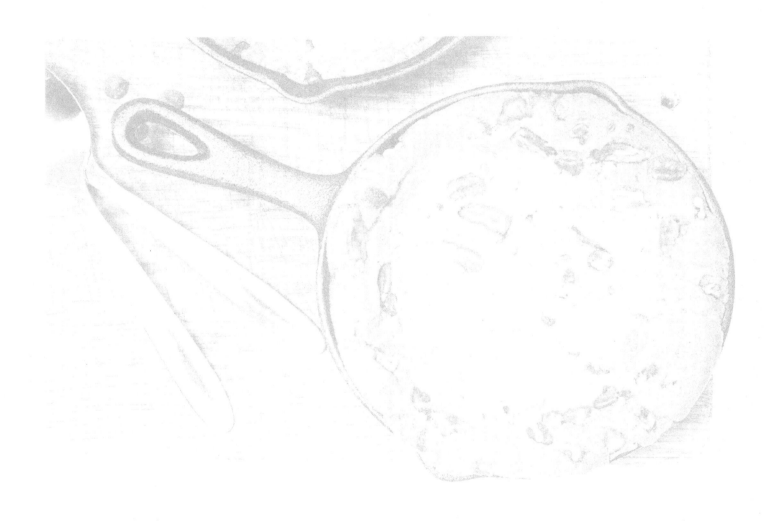

# CHAPTER 7:

## Recipes For Children

## 133.    **Rhubarb Cobbler**

⚜*Children use their senses a lot even when they eat. In the recipes, use many colors and excellent scents and you will conquer your children*⚜

**Difficulty Level:** Easy
**Servings:** 8
**Preparation Time:** 15 minutes
**Cooking Time:** 45 minutes
**Ingredients:**

- 4 c. rhubarb, chopped roughly
- ¾ c. light brown sugar
- 4 tbsp. butter, divided, melted, and cooled slightly
- ½ c. whole milk
- 2 large eggs, lightly beaten
- 1 tsp. vanilla extract
- 1½ c. all-purpose flour
- 2 tsp. baking powder
- 1 c. granulated white sugar

**Directions:**
1.    Preheat your oven to 350 °F. Arrange a rack in the center of the oven. Grease a cast-iron frying pan.
2.    Add the rhubarb and brown sugar to a large-sized bowl and toss to coat. Set aside.
3.    Add three tablespoons of butter, milk, eggs, and vanilla to another medium-sized bowl and stir to combine.
4.    Add the flour, baking powder, and sugar and with a whisk, stir until mixture becomes smooth and thick.
5.    Place the mixture into the prepared frying pan and spread evenly with the back of a spoon.
6.    Place the rhubarb over the mixture evenly and drizzle with the remaining melted butter.
7.    Bake for about 40-45 minutes until golden brown.
8.    Sprinkle with white sugar and serve warm.
**Nutrition (Per Serving):**
Calories: 319 Fat: 7.7g Carbohydrates: 59.5g
Fiber: 1.8g Sugar: 38.6g Protein: 5.1g

## 134.    **Nectarine Crisp**

⚜*Children taste new food slowly. Always give them healthy food. It will be a gift of health for them*⚜

**Difficulty Level:** Medium
**Servings:** 8
**Preparation Time:** 15 minutes
**Cooking Time:** 35 minutes
**Ingredients:**
For the Filling:

- 7 medium nectarines, cut into ¼-inch slices
- ¼ c. white sugar
- ¼ c. brown sugar
- ½ tsp. salt
- ½ c. caramel sauce
- ½ tsp. ground allspice

For the Topping:

- ¾ c. all-purpose flour
- ½ c. brown sugar
- ¼ tsp. ground allspice
- ¼ tsp. salt
- 6 tbsp. butter
- 1 c. gingersnap cookies, crumbled

**Directions:**
1.    Preheat your oven to 350°F. Generously grease a 12-inch cast-iron wok.
For filling:
2.    Add the nectarines, sugars, and salt to a large bowl and gently stir to combine. Set aside.
3.    For the topping: in a small-sized bowl, mix the flour, sugar, allspice, and salt.
4.    With a pastry blender, cut in butter until it is the size of peas.
5.    Stir in the gingersnaps and set aside.
6.    Drain the liquid from nectarines, leaving two tablespoons inside.
7.    Add the caramel sauce and allspice and gently stir to combine.
8.    Place the filling mixture into the prepared wok and sprinkle with the topping mixture.
9.    Bake for about 30-35 minutes or until the top becomes brown.
10.    Serve warm.
**Nutrition (Per Serving):** Calories: 396
Fat: 12.5g Carbohydrates: 70.6g Fiber: 3.4g
Sugar: 35.1g Protein: 6.2g

## 135.    Chocolate    Peanut    Butter    Cookie

*Peanut butter and chocolate are two ingredients that make every child happy*

**Difficulty Level:** Easy
**Servings:** 6
**Preparation Time:** 15 minutes
**Cooking Time:** 18 minutes
**Ingredients:**
- 1 c. all-purpose flour
- ⅓ c. unsweetened cocoa powder
- 1 tsp. cornstarch
- ½ tsp. baking soda
- ¼ tsp. salt
- ½ c. butter
- ½ c. white sugar
- ¼ c. brown sugar
- 1 egg
- 1 tsp. vanilla extract
- 1 c. peanut butter chips

**Directions:**
1.    Preheat your oven to 350°F. Generously grease a 9-inch cast-iron wok.
2.    Add the flour, cocoa powder, baking soda, cornstarch, and salt in a large bowl and mix well.
3.    In a medium-sized bowl, add the butter and sugars, and with an electric mixer, beat on medium speed until light and fluffy.
4.    Add eggs and vanilla extract and beat until well combined.
5.    Gently fold in the peanut butter chips.
6.    Place the dough into the prepared wok.
7.    Press the dough into an even layer with a spatula, leaving a ½-inch border around the edges.
8.    Bake for about 15-18 minutes or until the top is golden brown.
9.    Remove from the oven and set aside to cool for about 5 minutes before serving.

**Nutrition (Per Serving):** Calories: 535 Fat: 28.9g Carbohydrates: 63g Fiber: 4.1g Sugar: 38.8g Protein: 12.2g

## 136.    Apple Pie

*Apple pie is one of the oldest sweets that every grandmother has prepared for her grandchildren. Making it with cast iron is a new experience*

**Difficulty Level:** Easy
**Servings:** 10
**Preparation Time:** 15 minutes
**Cooking Time:** 32 minutes
**Ingredients:**
- 2 lbs. Braeburn apples, peeled, cored, and cut into ½-inch-thick wedges
- 2 lbs. granny smith apples, peeled, cored, and cut into ½-inch-thick wedges
- 1 tsp. ground cinnamon
- ¾ c. + 2 tbsp. white sugar
- ½ c. butter
- 1 c. brown sugar
- 2 pre-made pie crusts
- 1 egg white
- 2-3 tbsp. water

**Directions:**
1.    Preheat your oven to 350 °F.
2.    In a 10-inch cast-iron wok, melt butter over medium heat.
3.    Add the brown sugar and cook for about 1-2 minutes or until sugar is dissolved, stirring continuously.
4.    Remove from the heat and let the mixture cool. Add the apple wedges, ¾ c. of sugar, and cinnamon in a large-sized bowl and toss to coat.
5.    Arrange one pie crust in the wok over the brown sugar mixture.
6.    Now place the apple mixture over the bottom pie crust and cover with the remaining pie crust. Pinch the edges of both pie crusts slightly.
7.    Add the egg white and water in a small-sized bowl and beat until foamy.
8.    Brush the top crust with egg white mixture and sprinkle with remaining sugar with a pastry brush.
9.    Cut 4-5 slits on top of crust. Bake for about 60-70 minutes or until golden brown.
10.    Remove from the oven and place the pie onto a wire rack for about 30 minutes before serving.

**Nutrition (Per Serving):** Calories: 332 Fat: 14.9g Carbohydrates: 51.2g Fiber: 2.6g Sugar: 40.2g Protein: 1.8g

## 137.    Gingerbread Cake

❧*You teach your children to eat everything, even particular flavors and spices, but everyone likes gingerbread cake*❧

**Difficulty Level:** Easy
**Servings:** 8
**Preparation Time:** 15 minutes
**Cooking Time:** 40 minutes
**Ingredients:**
- 2 c. all-purpose flour
- ½ c. white sugar
- 2 tsp. ground ginger
- 1 tsp. ground cinnamon
- 1 tsp. baking soda
- ⅔ c. molasses
- ½ c. salted butter, melted
- 1 ⅓ c. buttermilk
- 1 large egg, beaten

**Directions:**
1.    Preheat your oven to 350°F. Grease and flour a 10-inch cast-iron wok.
2.    In a bowl, mix the flour, sugar, spices, and baking soda In another large-sized bowl, add the molasses and butter and beat well.
3.    Add the buttermilk and egg and beat until well combined.
4.    Add the flour mixture and mix well.
5.    Place the mixture into the prepared wok.
6.    Bake for about 35-40 minutes. When a toothpick that was inserted in the center comes out clean, the cake is done.
7.    From the oven, remove the wok and place it onto a wire rack to cool for at least 15 minutes before slicing.
**Nutrition (Per Serving):** Calories: 369 Fat: 12.9g Carbohydrates: 59.3g Fiber: 1.1g Sugar: 29.8g Protein: 5.5g

## 138.    Banana Cake

❧*In the cast iron you can also cook cakes. It is an excellent alternative to the traditional procedure*❧
**Difficulty Level:** Easy
**Servings:** 12
**Preparation Time:** 15 minutes
**Cooking Time:** 40 minutes
**Ingredients:**
- 2 c. all-purpose flour
- ¾ c. white sugar
- 1 tsp. baking soda
- 3 bananas, peeled and mashed
- 2 eggs
- ½ c. olive oil
- 3 tbsp. sour cream
- ½ c. walnuts

**Directions:**
1.    Preheat your oven to 350°F. Grease a 12-inch cast-iron wok.
2.    Add into a bowl the flour, sugar, and baking soda and mix well.
3.    Add the bananas, egg, oil, and sour cream to another large-sized bowl and beat until well combined.
4.    Stir in the flour mixture and mix until just combined.
5.    Gently fold in the walnuts.
6.    Place the mixture into the prepared wok.
7.    Bake for about 30-40 minutes. When a toothpick that was inserted in the center comes out clean, the cake is done.
8.    From the oven, remove the wok and place it onto a wire rack to cool for at least 10-15 minutes.
9.    Carefully place the cake upside down onto the rack to cool completely.
10.    Cut the cake into the desired sized slices and serve.
**Nutrition (Per Serving):** Calories: 278 Fat: 13.8g Carbohydrates: 35.9g Fiber: 1.7g Sugar: 16.3g Protein: 4.7g

## 139.    Cherry Clafoutis

❧*If your kids like cherries then make them this delicious recipe with cast iron*❧
**Difficulty Level:** Medium
**Servings:** 8
**Preparation Time:** 15 minutes
**Cooking Time:** 45 minutes
**Ingredients:**
- 1 tbsp. unsalted butter, softened
- ¾ c. whole milk
- ½ c. heavy cream
- 3 tbsp. Kirsch
- 2 tbsp. Amaretto
- 4 large eggs
- ½ c. + 2 tbsp. white sugar, divided

- ⅔ c. cake flour, sifted
- ¼ tsp. salt
- 3½ c. dark sweet cherries pitted

**Directions:**
1. Preheat your oven to 375°F. Generously grease a 10-inch cast-iron wok with the butter.
2. Add the milk, cream, liqueurs, eggs, and ½ c. of sugar in a blender and pulse well.
3. Mix in the flour and salt and pulse until well combined. Transfer the mixture into a bowl and set aside for about 5 minutes.
4. Place ⅓ of the mixture into the prepared wok and bake for about 5 minutes.
5. Remove from the oven and arrange the cherries on top, pressing them gently into the mixture. Sprinkle the cherries with the remaining two tablespoons of sugar, followed by the remaining flour mixture. Bake for about 35-45 minutes. When a toothpick that was inserted in the center comes out clean, the cake is done. From the oven, remove the wok and place it onto a wire rack to cool slightly before slicing.

**Nutrition (Per Serving):** Calories: 299 Fat: 7.7g Carbohydrates: 49.9g Fiber: 2.7g Sugar: 42.4g Protein: 6.4g

## 140.   Pear Cake

*❧Learn how to use your cast iron properly and you will get healthy food❧*

**Difficulty Level:** Easy
**Servings:** 8
**Preparation Time:** 15 minutes
**Cooking Time:** 45 minutes
**Ingredients:**
For the Cake Mixture:
- 2 c. all-purpose flour
- ½ c. granulated white sugar
- 2 tsp. baking powder
- 1 tsp. baking soda
- 1 tsp. ground cinnamon
- 2 eggs
- 1¼ c. buttermilk
- ½ c. butter, melted
- 2 tsp. vanilla extract

For the Pears:
- 4 c. pears, peeled, cored, and chopped
- ½ c. granulated white sugar
- ½ tsp. ground cinnamon

- ¼ tsp. ground nutmeg

**Directions:**
1. Preheat your oven to 350°F.
2. Grease a cast-iron wok.

For the Cake:
- Mix in a large-sized bowl the flour, sugar, baking powder, baking soda, and cinnamon.
3. Add the eggs, buttermilk, butter, and vanilla extract and mix until well combined.

For the Pears:
4. Add the pear slices, sugar, cinnamon, and nutmeg to another bowl and toss to coat well. The bottom of the prepared wok is spread half of the cake mixture. Place half of the pears on top of the cake mixture and top with the remaining cake mixture. Place remaining pears on top evenly.
5. Bake for about 40-45 minutes. When a toothpick that was inserted in the center comes out clean, the cake is done. From the oven, remove the wok and place it onto a wire rack to cool for at least 15 minutes. Cut the cake into the desired sized slices and serve.

**Nutrition (Per Serving):** Calories: 346 Fat: 13.4g Carbohydrates: 51g Fiber: 3.5g Sugar: 22g Protein: 6.3g

## 141.   **Caramelized Pineapple**

*❧Some children learn to eat fruit through play. Never forget that you too were a child and that you have learned a lot through playing❧*

**Difficulty Level:** Easy
**Servings:** 6
**Preparation Time:** 10 minutes
**Cooking Time:** 16 minutes
**Ingredients:**
- ¼ c. butter

- 1 fresh pineapple, peeled and cut into large slices
- ¼ c. brown sugar
- ¼ tsp. ground cinnamon

**Directions:**
1. In a large-sized cast-iron wok, melt the butter over medium heat.
2. Place half of the pineapple slices and sprinkle with brown sugar.
3. Cook for about 3-4 minutes per side, basting with the utter occasionally.
4. Sprinkle with cinnamon and serve.

**Nutrition (Per Serving):** Calories: 166 Fat: 7.9g Carbohydrates: 25.9g Fiber: 2.2g Sugar: 20.8g Protein: 0.9g

## 142. Apple & Blackberry Cake

⚜*Excellent variant of apple pie. Grab your cast iron and go to work*⚜
**Difficulty Level:** Easy **Servings:** 5
**Preparation Time:** 15 minutes
**Cooking Time:** 28 minutes
**Ingredients:**
For the Filling:
- 2 tbsp. coconut oil
- 1 tbsp. coconut sugar
- 3 sweet apples, cored and cut into bite-sized pieces
- ½ tsp. ground cinnamon
- ¼ tsp. ground cardamom
- ⅛ tsp. ground cloves
- ⅛ tsp. ground ginger
- 1 c. frozen blackberries
For the Cake Mixture:
- ¾ c. ground almonds
- ½ tsp. baking powder
- 2 tbsp. coconut sugar
- Pinch of salt
- ¼ c. full-fat coconut milk
- 1 tbsp. coconut oil, melted
- 1 egg, beaten
- ½ tsp. vanilla extract

**Directions:**
1. Preheat your oven to 400°F. Add butter and coconut sugar over high heat in a cast-iron wok and cook for about 2-3 minutes, stirring continuously.
2. Mix in the apples and spices and cook for about 5 minutes, stirring continuously. Remove from the heat, then stir in the blackberries. Meanwhile, mix ground almonds, baking powder, coconut sugar, and salt in a bowl. In another bowl, add remaining ingredients and beat until well combined.
3. Add egg mixture into the ground almond mixture and mix until well combined.
4. Place the mixture over fruit mixture evenly
5. Bake for 15-20 minutes. When a toothpick that was inserted in the center comes out clean, the cake is done. From the oven, remove the wok and place it onto a wire rack to cool for at least 15 minutes. Cut the cake into the desired sized slices and serve.

**Nutrition (Per Serving):** Calories: 292 Fat: 19g Carbohydrates: 30.2g Fiber: 6.7g Sugar: 21.1g Protein: 5.1g

## 143. Berry Cobbler

⚜*Try all the recipes in the "Recipes for Children" section because everyone likes these delicious recipes, even the eternal "Peter Pan"*⚜
**Difficulty Level:** Easy
**Servings:** 6
**Preparation Time:** 15 minutes
**Cooking Time:** 25 minutes
**Ingredients:**
- 3 c. fresh strawberries, hulled and halved
- 1½ c. fresh blueberries
- 1½ c. fresh raspberries
- ⅔ c. + 1 tbsp. white sugar, divided
- 3 tbsp. quick-cooking tapioca
- 1 c. all-purpose flour
- 2 tsp. baking powder
- ¼ tsp. salt
- ¼ c. cold butter, cubed
- 1 large egg
- ¼ c. + 2 tbsp. 2% milk
- 2-3 tbsp. coarse sugar

**Directions:**
1. Preheat your oven to 400°F. Grease a 10-inch cast-iron wok.
2. In a bowl, add the berries, ⅔ c. of sugar, and tapioca, and toss to coat well.
3. Place the berry mixture into the prepared wok evenly and set aside 20 minutes.
4. Meanwhile, mix the flour, one tablespoon of sugar, baking powder, and salt in a bowl.

5. With a pastry cutter, cut the butter until the mixture resembles coarse crumbs.

6. In another bowl, add the egg and milk and beat well.

7. Mix in the egg mixture into the flour mixture until just combined.

8. Place the flour mixture over berries in dollops with a tablespoon and sprinkle with coarse sugar.

9. Bake for is about 20-25 minutes or until the top becomes golden brown.

10. Serve warm.

**Nutrition (Per Serving):** Calories: 346 Fat: 9.6g Carbohydrates: 63.5g Fiber: 4.9g Sugar: 32.5g Protein: 4.9g

# 144. Plum Upside-Down Cake

*❧Take care of your cast iron. Periodically reheat some of the grease inside and remember to never wash it in the dishwasher. Some modern cast iron pans, however, can be washed in the dishwasher, always see the manufacturer's instructions❧*

**Difficulty Level:** Medium
**Servings:** 6
**Preparation Time:** 20 minutes
**Cooking Time:** 45 minutes
**Ingredients:**
- ⅓ c. butter
- ½ c. brown sugar
- 2 lbs. medium plums, pitted and halved
- 2 large eggs
- ⅔ c. white sugar
- 1 c. all-purpose flour
- 1 tsp. Baking powder
- ¼ tsp. Salt
- ⅓ c. hot water
- ½ tsp. lemon extract

**Directions:**
1. Preheat your oven to 350°F.
2. In a 10-inch cast-iron wok, melt the butter over medium-low heat and remove it from the heat.
3. Sprinkle brown sugar over butter evenly.
4. Arrange the plum halves over sugar in a single layer, cut side down. Set aside.
5. Mix together the flour, baking powder, and salt in a bowl.
6. Add in the eggs and beat the thick and lemon-colored in another large-sized bowl.

7. Slowly add the sugar and beat well.

8. Add the flour mixture and mix well.

9. Add the water and lemon extract and beat until well combined.

10. Place the flour mixture over plums evenly.

11. Bake for 40-45 minutes. When a wooden skewer or toothpick that was inserted in the center comes out clean, the cake is done.

12. From the oven, remove the wok and place it onto a wire rack to cool for at least 15 minutes.

13. Cut the cake into the desired sized slices and serve.

**Nutrition (Per Serving):** Calories: 331 Fat: 12.2g Carbohydrates: 53.2g Fiber: 0.9g Sugar: 36.5g Protein: 4.5g

# 145. Chocolate Cake

*❧Some dishes do not need to be commented on, but only to be tasted❧*

**Difficulty Level:** Hard
**Servings:** 6
**Preparation Time:** 15 minutes
**Cooking Time:** 30 minutes
**Ingredients:**
- 1 c. all-purpose flour
- 1 c. white sugar
- ½ c. brown sugar
- ½ c. cocoa powder
- 1½ tsp. baking powder
- ¾ tsp. salt
- ½ c. half-and-half
- ¼ c. butter, melted
- 1 tsp. pure vanilla extract
- 1 c. hot brewed coffee

**Directions:**
1. Preheat your oven to 350 °F. Lightly grease a 9-inch cast-iron wok.
2. Mix the flour, sugars, cocoa powder, baking powder, and salt in a large-sized bowl.
3. Add the half-and-half butter and vanilla extract in a medium-sized bowl and mix well.
4. Add the butter mixture to the bowl of the flour mixture and mix until just combined.
5. Place the mixture into the prepared wok and spread into an even layer with the back of a spoon.
6. Drizzle the top with coffee evenly.

7. Bake for 25-30 minutes. When a wooden skewer or toothpick that was inserted in the center comes out clean, the cake is done.
8. From the oven, remove the wok and place it onto a wire rack to cool for at least 10-15 minutes.
9. Carefully place the cake upside down onto the rack to cool completely.
10. Cut the cake into the desired sized slices and serve.

**Nutrition (Per Serving):** Calories: 360 Fat: 11.2g Carbohydrates: 66.6g Fiber: 2.7g Sugar: 45.4g Protein: 4.2g

## 146.   Brownie Pie

*A famous cake but preparing it with cast iron is another experience*
**Difficulty Level:** Easy
**Servings:** 6
**Preparation Time:** 15 minutes
**Cooking Time:** 30 minutes
**Ingredients:**
- ½ c. all-purpose flour
- ⅓ c. cocoa powder
- ¼ tsp. salt
- 1 c. white sugar
- ½ c. butter, melted
- 2 large eggs
- 1 tsp. vanilla extract
- ½ c. pecans, chopped

**Directions:**
1. Preheat your oven to 350°F. Grease a 9-inch cast-iron wok.
2. In a bowl, mix the flour, cocoa powder, and salt.
3. In another large-sized bowl, add the sugar and butter and beat well.
4. Add in vanilla and the eggs; beat well.
5. Add flour mixture and mix until well combined.
6. Gently fold in the pecans.
7. Place the mixture into the prepared wok evenly.
8. Bake for about 25-30 minutes.
9. Serve warm.

**Nutrition (Per Serving):** Calories: 407 Fat: 25.1g Carbohydrates: 45.6g Fiber: 3g Sugar: 34g Protein: 5.4g

## 147.   Blueberry Cobbler

*We prepare cakes for our children and remember to always use quality ingredients*

**Difficulty Level:** Easy
**Servings:** 8
**Preparation Time:** 15 minutes
**Cooking Time:** 25 minutes
**Ingredients:**
- 3 large eggs
- 1 c. whole milk
- ½ c. white whole-wheat flour
- ¼ c. + 1 tbsp. white sugar, divided
- ¼ tsp. salt
- ½ tsp. vanilla extract
- 2 tbsp. butter, melted
- 2½ c. frozen blueberries

**Directions:**
1. Preheat your oven to 400 °F. Grease a 9-inch cast-iron wok.
2. Add the eggs, milk, flour, ¼ c. of sugar, salt, and vanilla extract in a blender, and pulse until smooth.
3. Add butter and pulse for about 30 seconds more.
4. Place blueberries in the bottom of prepared wok evenly and top with flour mixture.
5. Dust with the remaining sugar evenly.
6. For about 25 minutes, bake, or wait until the top is golden brown.
7. Serve warm.

**Nutrition (Per Serving):** Calories: 150 Fat: 6g Carbohydrates: 20.9g Fiber: 1.8g Sugar: 14g Protein: 4.7g

## 148.    Glazed Banana

❧*A quick dessert to prepare but excellent to taste*❧

**Difficulty Level:** Easy
**Servings:** 2
**Preparation Time:** 10 minutes
**Cooking Time:** 8 minutes
**Ingredients:**
- 2 ripe bananas, peeled and cut into ½-inch thick slices
- 1 tbsp. butter
- 2 tbsp. honey
- ½ tsp. Ground cinnamon
- ⅛ tsp. salt

**Directions:**
1.    Add the butter, honey, cinnamon, and salt over medium heat and stir to combine in a cast-iron wok.
2.    Add in the banana slices and let each side cook for 2-3 minutes or until caramelized.
3.    Serve warm.

**Nutrition (Per Serving):**
Calories:  221
Fat: 6.2g
Carbohydrates:  44.7g  Fiber:  3.4g  Sugar:  31.7g
Protein: 1.4g

## 149.    Chocolate Chip Cookies

❧*With this recipe, I finished my work. I hope you and your whole family enjoy this recipe collection. Good Work*❧

**Difficulty Level:** Medium
**Servings:** 6
**Preparation Time:** 15 minutes
**Cooking Time:** 20 minutes
**Ingredients:**
- 1 c. all-purpose flour
- ½ tsp. baking soda
- ¼ tsp. coarse salt
- 6 tbsp. unsalted butter softened
- ½ c. granulated white sugar
- ⅓ c. dark brown sugar
- 1 large egg
- 1 tbsp. pure vanilla extract
- 1 c. semisweet chocolate chips

**Directions:**
1.    Preheat your oven to 350°F.
2.    Mix together the flour, baking soda, and salt in a bowl.
3.    In another large-sized bowl, add the butter and sugars, and with a wooden spoon, mix until smooth.
4.    Put in the egg and vanilla extract; mix well.
5.    Then, add the flour mixture and mix until just combined.
6.    Gently fold in the chocolate chips.

7.    Place the mixture into a 10-inch cast-iron wok, and with the back of a spoon, smooth the top surface.

8.    For 18-20 minutes, let it bake, or wait until the top is golden brown.

9.    Remove from the oven and set aside to cool for about 5 minutes before serving.

**Nutrition (Per Serving):** Calories: 471 Fat: 23.2g Carbohydrates: 64.7g Fiber: 2.6g Sugar: 43.4g Protein: 3.3g

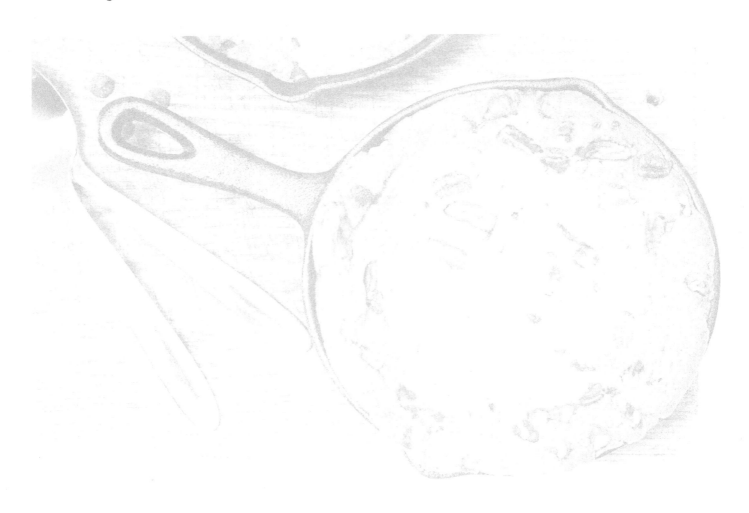

# CHAPTER 8:

## 30-Day Meal Plan

*⚜This meal plan will help you combine the recipes for your days, but you can create a number of other meal plans to your liking⚜*

| DAYS | BREAKFAST | LUNCH | DINNER |
|---|---|---|---|
| 1 | Milky Cornbread | Chicken Parmigiana | Sardines with Hearts of Palm |
| 2 | Bran Bread | Ground Turkey & Pasta Stew | Stuffed Salmon |
| 3 | Oat Pancakes | Ground Beef with Mushrooms | Shrimp Casserole |
| 4 | Tuna Omelet | Chicken with Pears | Seared Stuffed Trout |
| 5 | Eggs in Bell Pepper Rings | Pork Chops in Mushroom Sauce | Seafood Skillet Roast |
| 6 | Apple Pancakes | Chicken with Cabbage | Seasoned Tilapia |
| 7 | Oats Bread | Taco Ground Turkey | Lemony Cod with Capers |
| 8 | Cheddar Scramble | Moroccan Steak with Roasted Pepper Couscous | Salmon with Couscous |
| 9 | Sausage & Cauliflower Casserole | Chicken Marsala | Spicy Shrimp with White Beans and Tomatoes |
| 10 | Caramelized Figs with Yogurt | Chicken with Capers Sauce | Spicy Salmon |
| 11 | Chicken & Zucchini Pancakes | Turkey with Mushrooms | Zesty Salmon |
| 12 | Caraway Seed Bread | Chicken with Fig Sauce | Lemony Trout |
| 13 | Sourdough Bread | Parmesan Chicken Thighs | Halibut with Leeks and Carrots |
| 14 | Simple Bread | Simple Chicken Thighs | Herb Crusted Salmon |
| 15 | Hash Brown Casserole | Roasted Chicken with Leeks | Honey Mustard Salmon |
| 16 | Eggs in Tomato Cups | Mushrooms with spinach | Cabbage with Apple |
| 17 | Eggs in Beef Sauce | Chicken with Bell Peppers & Pineapple | Parmesan Quinoa & Asparagus |
| 18 | Bacon & Potato Scramble | Spiced Sirloin Steak | Mushroom with Spinach |
| 19 | Salmon Scramble | Steak with Green Veggies | Ratatouille |
| 20 | Veggies Omelet | Glazed Filet Mignon | Chickpeas Chili |
| 21 | Chicken & Asparagus Frittata | Tomatoes Braised Beef | Summer Squash Gratin |
| 22 | Sausage, Bacon & Potato Frittata | Ground Turkey with Lentils | Glazed Veggies & Apple |
| 23 | Spinach Frittata | Strip Steaks with Smoky Cilantro Sauce & Roasted Vegetables | Veggies Pie |
| 24 | Eggs in Sausage & Tomato Sauce | Cast-Iron Burgers | Herbed Bulgur Pilaf |
| 25 | Shakshuka | Steak with Chermoula | Creamy Zucchini Noodles |
| 26 | Hoisin Rib-Eye Steak | Steak with Glazed Carrots & Turnips | Zucchini Noodles with Mushroom Sauce |
| 27 | Eggs with Avocado and Spicy Tomatoes | Beef Tenderloin Steaks and Balsamic Green Beans | Broccoli with Cauliflower |
| 28 | Huevos Rancheros | Beef, Mango & Veggie Curry | BBQ Baked Beans |
| 29 | Eggs, Spinach & Mushrooms in a Skillet | Orange Glazed Steak | Beans & Quinoa with Veggies |
| 30 | Eggs with Crispy Potatoes and Green Beans | Fajitas with Chimichurri | Carrots with Snow Peas |

# Conclusion

Are you prepared to put your cast iron cookware to good use?

The dishes in this cookbook will undoubtedly be of assistance. Cast iron pans are a terrific and easy method to prepare a variety of meals since they can be used in the oven, on stovetops, on a grill, or even over a campfire to cook anything you want.

Their heavy-duty cast-iron bases make them ideal for all sorts of cooking. Keeping these characteristics in mind, we have produced a comprehensive collection of recipes for you to utilize, whether cooking at home or preparing wonderful meals outside.

Cast iron pans are not only sturdy but also long-lasting.

So, when you invest in cast-iron cooking equipment, you get long-term rewards. It's about time you got yourself a cast iron pan and started cooking with it!

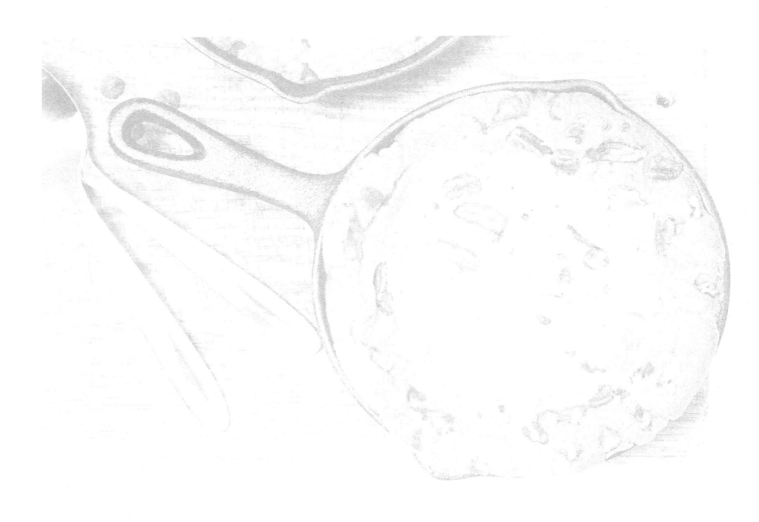

# Conversion Tables

## Volume Equivalents (Liquid)

| US STANDARD | US STANDARD (OZ.) | METRIC (APPROXIMATE) |
|---|---|---|
| 2 tbsp. | 1 fl. oz. | 30 mL |
| ¼ c. | 2 fl. oz. | 60 mL |
| ½ c. | 4 fl. oz. | 120 mL |
| 1 c. | 8 fl. oz. | 240 mL |
| 1½ c. | 12 fl. oz. | 355 mL |
| 2 c. or 1 pt. | 16 fl. oz. | 475 mL |
| 4 c. or 1 qt. | 32 fl. oz. | 1 L |
| 1 gallon | 128 fl. oz. | 4 L |

## Volume Equivalents (Dry)

| US STANDARD | METRIC (APPROXIMATE) |
|---|---|
| ¼ tsp. | 1 mL |
| ½ tsp. | 2 mL |
| 1 tsp. | 5 mL |
| 1 tbsp. | 15 mL |
| ¼ c. | 59 mL |
| ⅓ c. | 79 mL |
| ½ c. | 118 mL |
| 1 c. | 177 mL |

## <u>Oven Temperatures</u>

| Errore. Il segnalibro non è definito.FAHRENHEIT (F) | CELSIUS (C) (APPROXIMATE) |
|---|---|
| 250°F | 120 °C |
| 300°F | 150°C |
| 325°F | 165°C |
| 350°F | 180°C |
| 375°F | 190°C |
| 400°F | 200°C |
| 425°F | 220°C |
| 450°F | 230°C |

# Recipes Index

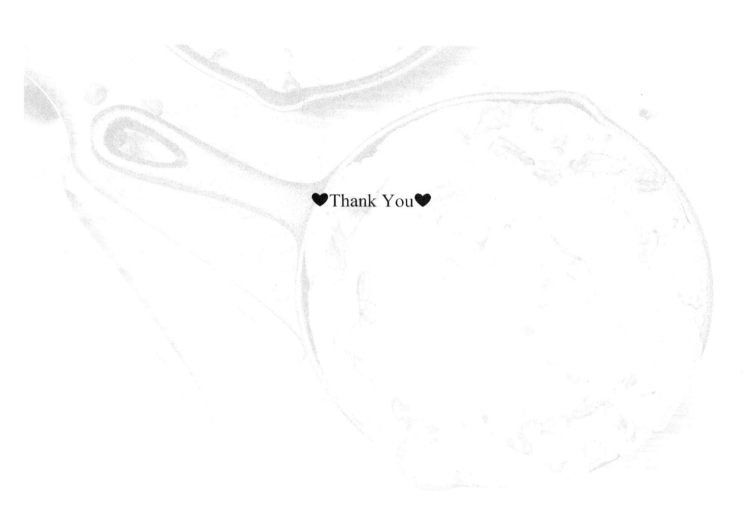

♥Thank You♥

Printed in Great Britain
by Amazon

79709826R00061